ARCHITECTURE AND THE CHURCH

ARCHITECTURE AND THE CHURCH

by the Commission on Church Architecture of
The Lutheran Church — Missouri Synod

BERNARD W. GUENTHER, A. I. A., Chairman

UEL. C. RAMEY, A. I. A., Secretary

WALTER R. HAGEDOHM, A. I. A.

EDGAR A. STUBENRAUCH, A. I. A.

KENNETH E. WISCHMEYER, F. A. I. A.

THE REV. ADOLF STIEMKE, Adviser

THE REV. ELMER E. STREUFERT, Adviser

Concordia Publishing House, St. Louis

Concordia Publishing House, St. Louis, Missouri
Concordia Publishing House Ltd., London, W. C. 1
© 1965 Concordia Publishing House

Library of Congress Catalog Card No. 65-22698

MANUFACTURED IN THE UNITED STATES OF AMERICA

PREFACE

The church will abide when all human structures crumble. Buildings may fail to weather the onslaught of civic changes or the ravages incidental to war and public disfavor. We need to distinguish between the concept of God's revelation of the church in Holy Writ and the usual interpretation men attach to a church as a location of public or private worship. Too frequently we forget the spiritual aspect of the church as the "communion of saints," something Almighty God has ordained as indestructible, because the risen Christ is the "Chief Cornerstone" (Eph. 2:20-22). Faith grants us entrance into this "body of Christ" and is undergirded by the promises of man's Redeemer. When man builds a church, its fabric is not the same as that which God employs. This accounts for the "mortality" of churches. God's foundation rests on the all-sufficient merits of Jesus Christ. Man raises a place of worship, prepared from "corruptible things," yet whose primary purpose is to aid the believer in acknowledging the Creator's supremacy and in humbly lauding the infinite mercy of our Lord as His Holy Spirit grants us grace to accept the fruits of Christ's reconciling atonement. In God's church nothing "shall be able to separate us from the love of God which is in Christ Jesus our Lord." However, in the structure that man designs, the "glory of God" may depart and they that congregate may be robbed of the truth that sanctifies in the sight of God, even though the building had at one time been dedicated for Christian services. It is true that when God's children "enter to worship" a world of strife is shut out and the wealth of His peace should abide within believing hearts, but we dare not confuse that thought with the idea that what one generation has built to further worship must, of necessity, endure all the encroaching forces of time.

It is logical that a book of this nature, presented for your consideration, should preface the presentation with the grounds that warrant its preparation. From the time of its organization our commission has recognized the need of offering guidelines to those who contemplate the development of churches and educational buildings. In previous years we have prepared brochures designed to help committees that seek proper guidance, especially in long-range planning, and to aid them toward avoiding costly and needless mistakes. Since these brochures were for free distribution, they were limited in scope in the interest of economy. Numerous requests for an expansion of their contents have led to the compilation of this book.

All the authors of the chapters are architects, members of the American Institute of Architects, and recognized for their ability in their chosen vocation. Each of the writers is governed by a deep sense of personal responsibility, the compulsion of reverence to strive always to honor our Triune God and never to be swayed in recommendations by opportunism. God demands, "Give Me thine heart" — an absolute consecration. Therefore only the best ought to be offered to the Lord's service and must remain the goal of aspiration. As the apostle admonished, "Whatsoever things are true, whatsoever things are honest, whatsoever things are lovely . . . think on these things." This requirement is fulfilled in more than our faithfulness to God's inspired communication to us in His sacred Word. It reaches into the administration of the means of grace our Lord has provided. It extends into the heritage of Christendom as it applies to the liturgy and education of the souls entrusted to pastoral care. It includes the adornment of God's house, making us aware that the iconography and symbolism we use ought never be in conflict with Holy Writ. It urges all to use the talents God has loaned as a sacred trust so that we always build according to means and never measure God's kingdom by our meanness or smallness of faith. It calls for an exercise of stewardship that includes a master plan for the growth God is able to bestow, rather than for a mere provision of the needs of a single generation of members. It embraces a prayerful approach to God's throne of grace, since He is able to do "exceeding abundantly above all that we ask or think." It observes God's admonition, "Whatsoever thy hand findeth to do, do it with all thy might." It reaches into the spreading of the light of the glorious Gospel "while it is day; the night cometh when no man can work."

The authors make no pretense that this book is the final word on the subject. Neither are the buildings used in illustration the ultimate in refinement, nor are they to serve as copies for duplication. Nor is there the presumption that this book contains the perfect answer for every individual problem. That is why the chapters specifically urge congregations to secure the able guidance of a qualified architect and not to resort to their own ingenuity, even though our forefathers hewed out their own log churches. Present day laws and codes are not designed to curb craftsmanship; they are safety restrictions.

In all humility we profess, "Thine is the glory!" Whatever is presented, that may be found praiseworthy, is but a reflection of the lasting praise that belongs to the "Giver of every good and perfect gift." It is our sincere petition that this volume may stimulate the reader to do the finer, ennobling things that are due His wondrous name.

So we built . . .
for the people had a mind to work.

A. J. Stiemke
E. E. Streufert

CONTENTS

ARCHITECTURE AND THE CHURCH

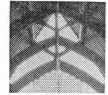

Chapter 1

CHURCH DESIGN

More has been written about church buildings, their historical background, their design, their construction and their financing, than about any other building type with the possible exception of school buildings. With so much literature available, it hardly seems necessary to write more. However, the most influential elements of church design have barely been mentioned, i. e., theology, doctrine, the symbolism of doctrine and liturgy.

A complete treatise on doctrine and its symbolism is not possible or even necessary in a book of this type. To write intelligently and in detail on these subjects would require that they be set forth within the framework of each particular denomination. Therefore it will be the purpose of this chapter to treat these subjects in rather broad general terms. For the most part they will be related to the liturgical church, with occasional reference to the nonliturgical denominations.

This chapter will contain no reference to specific buildings or their architects. All too often a published picture of a building may stamp that particular building as being outstanding in design and worthy of copying. If it should portray an excellent design, the same building erected at a different time, in a different place, and for a different set of conditions would be a mistake. If it should illustrate a poor example of architecture, this book would be misleading its readers.

It would be presumptuous to attempt to tell an architect how to design a church building. A competent architect needs no such instruction. Nor is it necessary for a congregation to be instructed in the art and science of architectural design. However, both the architect and the congregation need instruction in how to prepare themselves for the mutual task of creating a church structure.

Before undertaking a church building program, each congregation should make a thorough study of its theology, its doctrine, and its liturgy. This study should also encompass evaluation and interpretation, as well as understanding. In all probability, an objective study will strengthen the convictions of a congregation in these matters. A conscientious architect will require his client to preface the building program with clear and concise statements of the congregation's theology, an enumeration of its chief points of doctrine, and an explanation of its liturgy. The congregation should not assume that the architect has this knowledge and understanding. Nor should the architect reach the convenient conclusion that a church is simply another simple creation of masonry and mortar.

The architect must know and understand the theology, doctrines, and liturgy of his client. This may require research into the origin of the denomination to which his client belongs. The major non-Catholic Christian denominations in the Western Hemisphere can trace their origins back to the Protestant Reformation and to such men as Zwingli, Knox, Calvin, Huss, Wesley, Luther, and others. The architect may find, to his surprise, that it falls to his lot to lead his client in a study of theology as understood by his denominational affiliation. If this should be the case, the architect should be the leader, asking questions that require concise answers. It is not easy to translate a theology into a building that symbolizes theological background. Creating a symbol for an abstract thought requires philosophical insight. Few architects have this gift. The self-affixed title "Specialist in Church Architecture" is no guarantee that an architect has been blessed with so rare a talent.

There are three basic theologies in Western Christendom, i. e., the Roman Catholic, Lutheran, and the Reformed. The differences lie in teachings regarding the means of grace. In the broad concept Roman Catholic theology places greatest emphasis on the sacraments as the means of grace. Reformed theology is at the opposite end of the scale, where the preaching of the Word of God is considered the most essential means of grace with the sacraments of lesser relative importance. Lutheran theology falls between these two extremes, with equal emphasis being placed on Word and sacrament.

The liturgy will vary among congregations within the three basic theological groups. There is, however, very little variation in liturgy within Catholic, Episcopalian, and Lutheran worship. Liturgy becomes important to the designer because it determines the space requirements, the furnishings, the arrangement of the furnishings, as well as many other details. Whether it is complex or simple, it adds dignity, beauty, and spiritual significance to a worship service. Liturgy is often borrowed from one religious group and incorporated into that of another.

Doctrine is not so freely exchanged. Unfortunately, liturgy is frequently mistaken for doctrine. The church should be designed to accommodate the liturgy but, more important, it should symbolize the doctrines of the denomination. Therefore there should be distinct differences in the buildings of the three basic theological groups.

As a rule in a church for a Reformed denomination the focal point is the pulpit. The Communion table and choir are secondary and should not, in their design or placement, overshadow it. The introduction of an altar, with proper paraments and eucharistic candles would, in most cases, be considered inappropriate.

In a liturgical church, where the altar and the cross symbolize the throne of grace, to which each individual Christian has access through Jesus Christ, these elements become the focal point of the worship area.

The symbolical meaning of a church building is one of its most important functions. This may be the one quality which distinguishes it from any other building. The church building should not be expected to symbolize each and every minute point of doctrine of a denomination but it should express the basic beliefs.

How can some of these elementary beliefs be expressed in a building?

The traditional "in-line" or basilica plan is symbolic of the church militant. The Christian church is "fighting the good fight of faith." It is fighting this battle with the "armor of righteousness." The worshipers are arranged in ranks like an army. Their general, Christ, is in front, leading them onward. The modern church is still the church militant.

All Christian churches believe in the crucifixion, resurrection, and ascension of our Lord Jesus Christ. A cross, with or without corpus, standing in the midst of the congregation or held up in front of it, is a most effective way of representing this basic belief. This same cross, held high on a tower or firmly anchored in the churchyard, also preaches this message to the world.

Baptism, accepted by all Christians, needs to be more effectively represented in the church building. The small movable font, purchased from a church supply house, is hardly an adequate symbol for the sacrament that cleanses and regenerates man.

During the fourth, fifth, and sixth centuries, when the entire pagan and primitive world was brought into the church, baptism was recognized in its full significance, and the church plans of the day were arranged accordingly.

Baptismal proceedings took place in full view in the church entrance courtyard or atrium. Literally, a soul could not enter the church until baptismal ceremonials had been performed.

Spiritually, the same holds true today. But symbolically the significance is missing. The atrium has, for a variety of reasons, historic and economic, been reduced to an entrance vestibule or narthex, and the baptismal font has lost its grand tradition and been reduced to an item of furniture.

Baptism is not a sentimental act; therefore the baptismal font should be prominently displayed and of such proportions and detail as to give it and the sacred rite of Holy Baptism proper significance.

A Christian believes that he is "in the world" but not "of the world." His house of worship should express this belief. The building wherein he worships should isolate him, both physically and spiritually, from the world. The church should be the one place where the Christian feels the nearness of God to the exclusion of the world. Beauty must replace ugliness. Distracting activities and noises must be excluded. This does not imply that a church must be a windowless, uninviting, tomblike structure. On the contrary, it should be the most inviting of buildings. Its doors should say to the sinner, both Christian and heathen, that these are the doors to peace, to freedom, to joy, to a more abundant life, to quietness and rest.

The setting of the church should be such as will prepare the worshiper for entrance into the house of God and ease his transition from the house of God back into the world. It should encourage him to come often. The doctrine of the Holy Trinity can be symbolized in this area. The sky and earth are reminders of God the Father; the cross, of God the Son; and the evidence of fellowship, of God the Holy Spirit.

In recent years "the church in the round" has made its appearance again. This plan is an excellent symbol for Christian theology. A congregation is a family of believers. This is a real thing. Christians are brothers and sisters in Christ. Members of "the household of faith" feel a deep concern for each other. They share each other's joys and sorrows. The strong in faith encourage the weak. Those who have understanding instruct those who lack understanding. The act of corporate worship strengthens faith. Christ said, "Where two or three are gathered together in My name, there am I in the midst of them." The congregation encircling the altar symbolizes this communion of saints.

The circular plan dates back to the earliest days of the Eastern church. It was developed to a high degree during the Byzantine era, spreading rapidly to the entire Mediterranean area and southern Europe. The circle denotes the oneness of God and eternity under God.

The contemporary adoption of the circular plan, which places altar and cross as a central focal point, is perhaps more logical than the original concept, which placed the chancel at the circumference and arranged the nave seating somewhat illogically without regard to the centralized nature of the plan.

Christ would have every Christian make a total commitment of his life to Him. "Love the Lord, thy God, with all thy heart, with all thy soul, with all thy mind, and with all thy strength." This commitment is one wherein the Christian lets Christ come into every thought and activity of his life. Christ becomes the very center, the heart and purpose in every Christian's life, not only in his worship and prayer but also in his work, recreation, and educational pursuits. The church building should express this centrality of Christ in the Christian's life. The cross is the commonly accepted symbol of Christ's love for man. If this symbol is a reminder of His love, its presence could project into the educational and recreational areas of the building, as well as the worship area.

Out of love, Christ sacrificed Himself for man. A Christian recognizes this. The Christian's gifts of love should be a sacrifice also. His church building should be a sacrificial gift of love, not only to God but also to one's children and grandchildren. A gift of love is not sham, imitation, or show. It is honest and sincere. It is given humbly. A church edifice ought to symbolize the Gospel of Christ's sacrificial love through honest construction, fineness of materials, and concern for detail.

A Christian believes that all that he has comes from God. His possessions are a trust to be used to the glory of God here on earth. Among these gifts are fine building materials, both new and old, the mental capacity to develop new and better techniques in building construction, imagination to develop new forms, and wisdom which can utilize these gifts in the construction of the house of God. Creative and appropriate use of materials, techniques, and forms is good stewardship and glorifies God.

A Christian congregation assembles (at least once each week) to worship the Lord in prayer and song and to be instructed in the Scriptures. This act of worship is participated in by all members, including the pastor and the choir. It is done to please God. Any part of this sacred act which is done to please the congregation or glorify man is not an act of worship. Vestments worn by the pastor are worn for the purpose of concealing the man so that God may be glorified through him. The purpose of a choir and organist is to lead the congregation in worshiping the Lord with music. The members of a choir and the organist should be subordinate to their offering of music. The choir sings, not for the entertainment of the congregation or for the glory of its members but rather to the glory of God.

Although man's nature has not changed, the conditions under which he lives have changed dramatically in the past centuries, and continue to change year by year. God has not changed and His Word is as timely today as in the past. His Gospel is contemporary. The buildings wherein this timeless Gospel is preached and taught should be contemporary. What significance can be attached to a 20th-century copy of a 14th-century Gothic church? Classic, Gothic, Renaissance, and Georgian architecture represented the way of life of a particular time. Do they represent the way of life of today? Some Christian congregations who have realized that they are living in the 20th century and that the Scriptures are contemporary have built beautiful modern churches.

Christianity is a religion of love ("Love the Lord, thy God . . . love thy neighbor"); it is a religion of hope and joy; it is a religion of beauty ("whatsoever things are beautiful . . ."); it is an active religion ("Go ye and teach all nations"); Christianity is enduring ("My Word shall not pass away"); it offers free salvation to everyone ("that whosoever believeth in Him should not perish but have everlasting life"). The buildings that house the true Christian spirit witness and symbolize these truths to all who use them and to those who only see them.

Chapter 2

THE BUILDING COMMITTEE

The use of a building committee as the responsible church body to control a building project is a time-honored democratic method employed for generations in most church denominations since the Reformation. It is a committee on which great responsibility rests, as its judgment, open-mindedness, business ethics, and common sense can many times actually determine the success or failure of a building project. Many congregations build only once in a generation, and too often they do not understand the importance and responsibility of the building committee when selecting its members. A few churches in America, and most of those in Europe, give complete control of their building program to an individual, a centralized architectural bureau, or a subdivision of the church. This brings results and centralizes responsibility but does not always lead to the best design solution.

The basic theory, therefore, of using a building committee is a good one, provided certain criteria are adhered to in the selection of the members. Most denominations prefer a broad representation on the committee, but frequently this results in an unwieldly number and sometimes the appointment of uninformed persons who are concerned exclusively with their own limited field. A good choice of members with a broad viewpoint and open-minded attitude, therefore, becomes essential.

The appointment of the building committee is usually made by the church council, the board of elders, or the voters' assembly and should be made only after deliberation and the thorough investigation of the persons considered for appointment. It

is to be noted that the committee should not be composed entirely of members actively engaged in the construction field. In fact, it is a serious mistake to limit the committee to those in this field.

Normally it is good practice to select a chairman with broad business experiences who has contacts with people, has a knowledge of finance, is ethical in his business practices, and is familiar with local governmental requirements and practices. The chairman's greatest asset should be his ability to mediate with common sense among various church organizations and groups, work harmoniously with his committee, and conduct all proceedings in a level-headed, broadminded, and fair manner. Too often architects and other professionals find a chairman who is narrow in his point of view, is loaded with preconceived ideas of what the project should be before a line is drawn, and who attempts to denominate the entire proceedings to the detriment of the success of the project. This type of person should be avoided under all circumstances, regardless of his personal standing in the church.

A general contractor is a good member to include as usually his broad experience and detailed construction judgment can be invaluable to a committee. However, a general contractor who intends to bid on the project should not be included among the committee members.

A civil, structural, or mechanical engineer is normally good material for membership, but here again his qualifications should be investigated to learn whether or not his background is broad enough.

A banker, savings and loan official, or some member working in the fiscal offices of an insurance company or business corporation is an excellent prospect. Such a member can bring a wealth of fiscal knowledge to the committee, highly essential to their deliberations and subsequent recommendations to the church body.

An educator at any level — elementary, secondary, or college — is considered a fine candidate as a committee member. Usually a man or woman with comprehensive educational background can contribute much to the educational function of the church and the ever-changing curriculum and physical space requirements necessitated by modern teaching practices.

A merchant or a farmer (if the church is located in a rural area) who has daily contact with people of all types provides a leaven to the membership in its dealings with various personalities and can augment the business knowledge of the other business-experienced members.

Too often men in specialized trades in the building industry, such as plumbers, brick masons, carpenters, plasterers, etc., are included as committee members. Although there may be exceptions to the rule, their restricted experience limits their overall concept of the problem. They, therefore, do not always make good building committee members.

Architects who are members of the congregation and are not selected to provide the professional services for the project do not usually make good members, unless they too are the exceptions to the rule and can be equally broad and objective in their deliberations and recommendations.

The pastor, of course, should be an ex-officio member. He is an important member for, although not voting in committee decisions, he brings his all-encompassing knowledge of his own parishioners and of the church's needs, as well as his general acceptance in the church's public relations with the community.

Other ex-officio members could be the assistant pastor (if it is a larger congregation), the director of religious education, and the Sunday school superintendent. Their inclusion would again depend on the total size of the committee and their personal abilities to make an additional contribution beyond the scope of the pastor.

A committee of five or seven is ideal and can function efficiently as a manageable group. This size committee can from a practical standpoint meet more frequently and advantageously with fewer people to accommodate on acceptable meeting dates. It can also develop a mutual respect for one another with more intimate exchange of ideas and viewpoints.

Large committees of from 10 to 20 members are usually unmanageable in their thinking and invariably bring about many compromise decisions leading to mediocre results, in an effort to please everyone. Some church boards, councils, elders, and voters' assemblies are under the erroneous impression that more heads make more sense and consequently reach a better solution. Unfortunately this is not true — the contrary situation prevails. So a group of from five to seven with the proper qualifications is an ideal building committee, with a usually normal construction program assured.

After its appointment the committee should be organized with either an appointed or elected chairman and secretary. The secretary should keep minutes of all of the proceedings and financial commitments so that an accurate record is kept for church files and references in order to prepare reports and recommendations to the church council, elders, or voters' assembly. All meetings should be conducted in a businesslike manner with decisions made in the form of a resolution and votes cast after deliberation. It is recommended that regular meeting nights be established so that committee members can arrange their calendars to insure regular attendance. Thus a properly organized committee can perform its duties with dispatch and insure a time-saving and smoothly developed program in normal stages.

It is always good practice for the appointing body — elders, church council, or voters' assembly — to define and limit the duties of the building committee in order to avoid overlapping of responsibilities and to inform the committee of exactly what the church body expects of it. The normal duties of a church building committee, whether it be for a church sanctuary, educational building, parochial school, parsonage, or for other construction programs, are to:

1. Determine the need to be considered, both for immediate construction and for a long-range program requiring a master plan. Usually this program is developed by all of the church's organizations with the assistance of the pastor and is done by a planning committee prior to the selection of a building committee.

2. Obtain, at the church's expense, a survey of the site including boundary lines, topography, location of trees, adjoining buildings, streets and curbs, building setback lines, and location of all utilities, such as sewer, water, gas, electric, and storm water.

3. Obtain copies of all zoning restrictions affecting the church property.

4. Secure copies of deed restrictions to determine site areas available for development, if the church is in a subdivision.

5. Obtain, at church expense, test borings of the soil. This should be done, however, only after the architect is engaged and the exact area on which the building is to be built is generally agreed on. It is wise to get this information in the preliminary sketch stage so that if any unusual soil condition exists it can quickly be determined whether or not this factor will affect the design solution.

6. Make available all plans, drawings, and surveys of existing buildings on the church property if the project is to be an alteration or an addition.

7. Select an architect if so empowered by the elders, church council, or voters' assembly. This is to be done by methods defined in the chapter "The Architect."

8. Approve the architect's contract for the proper church official's signature.

9. Give to the architect and discuss with him the church's total program, including the church's building program, together with the contemplated scope of immediate and long-range plans, including an idea of the church's financial capacity and an approximate budget from which the architect can work and advise the committee as to the budget's adequacy or inadequacy for the contemplated work.

10. Select one member of the committee, usually the chairman, as the spokesman to convey all instructions to the architect. The architect in turn can deliver reports, arrange meetings, inspections, and other pertinent business through him.

11. Prepare all necessary reports of progress and recommendations to the church body having authority.

12. Review all successive stages of development of the architect's plans, including structural and mechanical work, together with the specifications covering same.

13. Receive bids for construction after approval from the church's governing body to do so, if this is required under the scope of authority initially given to the building committee. Some church denominations require that all plans and specifications be reviewed and approved by their architectural department at each development stage. This procedure may cause some delays, but in general is not objectionable, as the review board is usually composed of competent professionals.

14. Recommend, with the approval of the architect, the general contractor and any subcontractors, if separate bids are received on such items as heating and air conditioning, plumbing, electric work, and church furnishings and equipment, to the church governing body.

15. Approve, after certification by the architect, construction contracts for signature, and review Labor and Material Payment Bond and Performance Bond, and contractor's insurance certificate for compliance.

16. Check progress of construction with the architect and expedite architect's certificates of contractor's monthly estimates for payment by the church treasurer or the financial institution designated by the church's governing body.

17. Make final check with the architect of the building and approve acceptance after all work is completed and all outstanding obligations are paid.

18. Prepare and submit to the church's governing body regular construction reports of progress and, after all duties are discharged, submit a final report.

19. The building committee should provide legal counsel for all contracted or legal matters at the congregation's expense. Insurance matters should be reviewed in detail.

From the above outline of committee duties one can see that it is fitting to state again that the building committee for any church building project has exacting responsibilities and should have full authority. The significance of qualified members is apparent.

The building committee should at all times operate on a high businesslike and ethical plane, consider all transactions as business transactions, and thus avoid putting the church's reputation in jeopardy by such practices as requesting concessions, discounts, cut rates, or reduced fees and withholding or delaying payments due the architect and contractor. Too often good community public relations, developed in a painstaking manner over many years, are ruined overnight by an inept building committee in its handling of the church's business. It also happens too often that members of a building committee who are actively engaged in the construction field have a double set of standards, one that they practice in their own work and the other on a more exacting scale that they apply to the inspection of work done by the contractors for the church's construction. This practice is unfair and unchristian and frequently brings the church's name into ill repute.

It is, therefore, essential that the building committee members guard against such practices and operate with truthfulness and with sincerity to conform to all high Christian standards, so that at all times they heed the ethics of good business conduct, adhere to contractual relationships, and approach their problems with Christian principles. It is only then that the work of the church with its serious attendant responsibilities can be accomplished efficiently and with Christian dignity.

Chapter 3

THE BUILDING PROGRAM

The development of a comprehensive activities program is the first major step that a church takes prior to proceeding with a building program and is usually done prior to the appointment of a building committee or the selection of an architect. After a congregation has determined to proceed with a building project, it is essential that a planning or program committee be appointed by the elders, church council, or voters' assembly. This committee, in contrast to the building committee, should be a large committee, embracing all segments of church life. It should function as a "fact-finding" group, with the vital statistics of the church — numbers, age groups, possible patterns of growth, financial history — as the background for the gathering of information pertaining to present and future needs and activities.

The activities committee should have a chairman, usually someone thoroughly familiar with the congregation and with an intimate knowledge of the church and its history. A past president of the congregation or a member of the board of elders or church council is a likely prospect for this responsible position. The other members of this committee should be:

1. Member of the board of elders, church council, or governing body
2. Member of the church finance board
3. Member of the Sunday school board
4. Member of the school board (if a parochial school exists)
5. Member of the women's guild or ladies' aid
6. Member of the choir or music committee
7. Member of the church maintenance or church properties board
8. Member of the young people's organization
9. Member of the married couples' group
10. Member of the adult Bible class group
11. Member of the altar guild
12. Member of the food service committee
13. Pastor of the congregation
14. Assistant pastor or director of religious education
15. A member of the congregation at large

The purpose of such a large committee is to determine detailed needs and activities of all phases of the complete church life so that all groups are given an opportunity to be heard, present their requirements, and feel that they are an integral part of the expansion program. Ignoring any single phase or group can be injurious to the ultimate success of the project, even though in the first submission of information much of it may be impractical, overly optimistic, too costly, idealistic, or unrealistic.

This total involvement has many direct and indirect benefits. It creates interest and enthusiasm, promotes unity, and generates support. It, therefore, becomes the responsibility of the activities committee to collect, organize, and compile all the activities and needs into a comprehensive program of church needs.

At a first indoctrination meeting of the committee, before any data are formulated and presented for consideration, the true current vital statistics of the congregation should be ascertained — such as:

1. Total number of souls by general age groups.
2. Total number of communicant members.
3. Total number of Sunday school enrollees.
4. Total active members.
5. Average church attendance.
6. Average Sunday school attendance — broken down into age groups.
7. Average parochial school attendance by grades.
8. Average yearly budget — last five years.
9. Average yearly member's contribution by categories.
10. Average yearly growth pattern by age groups.
11. List of all current activities with present equipment, membership, frequency of meetings, and other pertinent information.
12. All statistics should be projected for future growth.

It should be further determined in what type of community the church is located and what are prospects of future growth. To define this question it is helpful to have a city zoning and planning map that shows land use and accurate present and possible future growth patterns of the community. This should not be guesswork, although in setting up a growth pattern on past vital statistics and future five-year growth stages some estimates for the future will have to be determined for as far as perhaps 20 years.

Financial responsibility should be explored at this time and a realistic stewardship program should be discussed, bearing in mind the well-established fact that new and better facilities for church activities increase membership and stimulate giving.

At the indoctrination meeting the chairman should charge the members to develop their needs in detail, both immediate and future, with their respective boards, committees, and organizations, keeping in mind the vital statistics established and the general financial limitations of the congregation. A clear and concise statement of the philosophy of the congregation relating to the particular program of construction being considered should also be resolved at this initial meeting. This statement of philosophy is important because it is the framework within which the program is to be planned; it is the standard by which all needs are evaluated; it is the goal to be achieved.

The chairman should give ample time for the individual members of the committee to gather the necessary data, for the degree to which a building successfully houses the activities of a congregation depends to a very great extent on the thoroughness with which the program of activities and needs is prepared. Therefore good stewardship would dictate ample time to prepare the material for committee consideration and final evaluation.

Subsequent meetings of the committee should produce a vast amount of information and an extensive session may be scheduled, or a series of evening meetings, to give the proper thought and attention to the material at hand. It is then prudent to wait a week or 10 days to meet again to allow the members to evaluate in their own minds the many requests for areas and equipment to accommodate the activities of the congregation. It may then be wise to formulate the program on the basis of the five basic congregational activities, which are:

1. Worship
2. Education
3. Fellowship
4. Recreation
5. Administration

Each of these activities can be broken down into many subdivisions and the related data applied. It is worthy of note that the simpler the outline of the program, the more readily intelligible it will be to the congregation as a whole and, therefore, more easily acceptable for approval.

The final draft of the program should answer the following questions:

1. Is it realistic of accomplishment?
2. Have all groups, boards, and committees had their opportunity to be heard?
3. Is it compatible with budget limitations and future anticipated financial growth?
4. Does it anticipate future growth?
5. Does it conform to current church and educational standards?
6. Is it compatible with zoning and planning codes?
7. Does it anticipate change in area use?
8. Does it have the approval of all church activity groups?
9. Does it conform to the objectives of the denomination at large?

Should the program answer in the affirmative all

of the questions, it is then ready for final presentation to the congregation through the church governing body. At this stage the guidance of the building committee and the architect would be of great value. The method of presentation is important in order to obtain approval, and again a simple, direct, and concise method is recommended. Individual copies of the program can be given to each member present, or the program can be mailed a week in advance to give the congregation an opportunity to review the contents before attending the meeting.

Complete cooperation and enthusiasm of each member of the congregation is a great advantage to the implementation of the program in the hands of the newly appointed building committee, which will now assume the responsibility of its work. Some churches make the planning committee the building committee — a method to be discouraged, as their functions and membership qualifications are different.

The development of a well-thought-out and factual program is an essential ingredient of a successful building program. It should never be formulated in haste as an expediency to start construction or be considered as an unimportant point of the overall building project or projects. It is far better to plan with prudence than regret the mistakes for a generation.

Programming must be visionary and idealistic. It should tend toward the horizon. It should be objective, impersonal, and totally without rancor. Pressure groups belong in the political arena. There is no place for them in the church of Christ, and least of all during the programming period.

Little plans have no place in God's design for man, and certainly not in man's plans for God.

Chapter 4

THE ARCHITECT

Architecture is one of the oldest and most noble of the arts. Architecture is among the oldest of the professions. It is an authentic human record of history inscribed in countless buildings both of modest import and aspiring dimensions. The character of man's buildings reflects in true terms the civilization of the period. There is no escaping the great sweeping political, social, and religious upheavals of history as manifested in the architecture of their day. During the procession of history the church architect, who was really the master builder of his day, was in prominence or relative obscurity, depending on the impact of religion on the times. In all buildings that man has built on earth, his spirit, his pattern, rose great or small. It lived in his buildings. It still is evident. This great spirit, common to all buildings, is architecture.

The word *architect* is defined as "the deviser, maker, or creator of anything." This is a broad definition and has been used in the religious sense of God being the architect of the world, the political sense of public servants being the architects of international agreements, and so on. But the Greek word *architekton* meant "chief builder," and so we think of him today as the leader of the design and building team in the modern sense in any construction project.

The qualified architect of today is a man who has spent four to five years in training in a recognized and accredited architectural school and has served a training period in one or several architectural offices. The length of this training varies, with some even furthering their training by attending postgraduate schools or studying in foreign countries.

As in all professions, the level of competence required for adequate and satisfactory practice is constantly rising.

Within the last 10 years registration laws governing architectural practice have been enacted in the remainder of the 50 states of the Union. Such controls strengthen the requirements of architectural practice and increase the level of competence expected of the practitioner.

In a similar vein the length of architectural study in all architectural schools has been increased from four years to five, and the curriculum has been reviewed and progressively changed to meet present-day and future anticipated requirements. The curriculum has also been broadened to include the study of the humanities to produce well-rounded students who will develop into mature architects with a greater appreciation of the civilized components with which they will work.

To guide, control, and promote the architectural profession, the American Institute of Architects was founded in 1857 with the objective to organize and unite in fellowship the architects of the United States of America; to combine their efforts so as to promote the aesthetic, scientific, and practical efficiency of the profession; to advance the science and art of planning and building by advancing the standards of architectural education, training, and practice; to coordinate the building industry and the profession of architecture to insure the advancement of the living standards of our people through improving their environment; and to make the profession of ever-increasing service to society. Other parallel groups exist in all countries and have the same objectives.

The institute, recognizing that an architect must play the role of creative artist, sound constructor, professional adviser, business administrator, and impartial judge, has developed standards of professional practice. These, states the profession of architecture, call for men of the highest integrity, judgment, business capacity, and artistic and technical ability. The architect's honesty of purpose must be above suspicion, as the architect acts as an unprejudiced professional adviser to his client, as well as moderator between client and contractor. He also has moral responsibilities to his professional associates as well as responsibilities to the public. These duties and responsibilities cannot be properly discharged unless his motives, conduct, and ability are such as to command respect and confidence. The architect must guard the health and safety of the public.

The layman rarely comes in direct contact with architects and is unfamiliar with their methods of practice. The type and method of practice varies with the size of the architect's office, from the individual practitioner to the average office of from 4 to 8 men, to the medium office of 9 to 20, to the large office of from 20 to 100 and over. Offices of these various sizes fit into public requirements for architectural services to be rendered, but in general for the normal church or church educational project more personalized services can be obtained from all but the largest of the above-mentioned offices.

To understand the methods of practice, a complete summary of the architectural process is broken down into logical steps of development. They apply to all types of buildings, including churches, and the church-building group will do well to study and understand them. Such study will make working with the architect easier and will foster cooperation during the months of planning and constructing a new religious building.

The architect's functions in the building process have already been summarized as design and supervision, but fuller description is needed as a basis for more detailed consideration of current professional problems. Since the attainment of new facilities is the chief mission of the building process, it follows that architects are concerned with all projects.

In essence, the architectural process consists of five types of functions. First is the formulation of the problem to be solved, from the architect's view-point, which is expressed in the program. Second, the creation of the basic design solution. Third, the preparation of the working documents, the plans, specifications, and other instruments by which the proposed design can best be guided to successful realization. Fourth, administrative coordination, to promote the efficient operation of the process. Fifth, inspection and administration, by which accurate fulfillment of the drawings and specifications is verified and guided.

It is manifest that these functions are neither separate, isolated actions nor ends in themselves. Rather they unite to form an integrated, systematic, and time-tested method by which architects can focus their professional knowledge, skill, and judgment most effectively to serve their clients. These services, which form the normal method by which architects perform their functions for building projects, proceed in the following five normal stages.

A. Program Stage

On the basis of the needs, site, and available economic resources of the building project as presented by the parish, the architect gathers, collates, and integrates all data and conditions which determine the scope and character of the problem. After thorough investigation of these elements and their interrelationships, he organizes his findings in a definitive program.

The purpose of the program is to ensure initial agreement between client and architect regarding the problems to be solved so that subsequent stages can proceed logically and promptly. Frequently a congregation is able to conceive of its needs in only the vaguest terms. Some jump to unwarranted conclusions which disregard vital factors. In both cases the architect's counsel is an invaluable safeguard. Indeed, the more experienced the client, the more he values the fresh and independent view which an imaginative architect can contribute in his formulation of the basic program.

For small projects architects often find informal discussions with the client quite sufficient to produce an effective program. In recent years, however, for larger, more complex projects, and especially when group decisions are involved, many architects prepare elaborate formal programs.

B. Basic Design Stage

On the basis of the approved program, the architect develops studies leading to a basic solution acceptable to the client.

The basic design stage is the heart of the architectural process, for here are determined the actual form and character of the final building. It is here that skillful architects exhibit their superior creativeness in practical but imaginative plans, logical structures, sensitive spatial relationships, fresh and vigorous forms, and fineness of detail.

After thorough analysis of all pertinent aspects and components of the problem, in order to gain insight into its controls and potentialities, the architect synthesizes a number of tentative solutions in schematic form. In each, the necessities of site, codes, utilities, construction, equipment, operation, maintenance, attractiveness, and budget are carefully considered. All are tested for suitability, and perhaps combined or refined, until there emerges a solution satisfactory to both client and architect.

Once tentatively approved, this solution is further developed in greater detail until all aspects and parts join in harmonious unity. This basic design is then presented to the client by means of diagrams, drawings, and sometimes models, together with a report of recommendations describing salient features, specifying briefly the proposed materials, structural systems, and equipment, and providing a reliable estimate of the time and expenditures required for erection. The congregation's approval at this point establishes the basis necessary for subsequent work.

C. Working Documents Stage

In this stage the architect determines and records the means by which the basic design can best be brought to practical achievement. The delineations and descriptions which fix in detail the final building and the method of its execution comprise the working drawings and specifications, which together form the working documents, or instruments of service.

The working documents supplement and complement each other to define the desired building and its construction. The working drawings describe, by means of plans, elevations, sections, scale details, and schedules, the kind, size, form, location, and assembly of all materials, equipment, site work, and

decoration. For most but the simplest projects, the architectural drawings are supplemented by other sets showing the structural system and the mechanical, electrical, heating, ventilating, sanitary, and other special installations. The specifications describe the types, qualities, finish, and manner of placing of all materials and components. The general conditions, which are part of the supplement, set forth the rights and duties of client, architect, and contractor.

It should be noted that many questions of design can be answered intelligently only as the working drawings begin to take shape. Indeed, some types of design decisions often continue to be made even during actual construction. Conversely, since methods of construction greatly influence design, they must be considered, at least in general terms, during the basic design stage. Such overlapping simply emphasizes the unity of the whole architectural process.

It is manifest that the quality of the completed building depends not only on the excellence of its basic conception but also on the degree of skill with which it is constructed. It is axiomatic that no detail can be left to its own devices if a coordinated result is desired. Completeness, accuracy, and consistency are, therefore, utmost essentials for the working documents. Without these qualities it is difficult, if not impossible, to obtain accurate estimates, secure lowest fair market price, eliminate excessive contingency allotments in bids, or avoid extraordinary extra charges or costly delays in completing the project. With these qualities, however, the work can proceed expeditiously and with minimum friction. Since the presence of these qualities is synonymous with competence, it follows that an architect must be able and competent to stand personally responsible for the quality of service he performs.

D. Construction Contract Stage

Upon completion of the working documents, the architect advises and assists the client in selecting bidders, obtaining bids, and negotiating an equitable contract for the construction of the building.

This stage involves two steps: the selection of the contractor, and the negotiation of the construction contract. In the first step the architect advises the client as to the qualifications of those who are to be invited to submit bids, and the architect prepares the bid forms and notices, and issues them to those invited. Upon receipt of the proposals, the architect advises the client as to their acceptance. In the second step, after the client's acceptance of a contractor's proposal, the architect advises in the preparation of the terms, conditions, and forms of the construction contract and other accompanying instruments.

These phases of the architect's service are of great benefit to the congregation because they provide guidance and protection in a highly complex technical transaction. In selecting the contractor, for example, it must be recognized that no contract can ever insure a quality of work for which the contractor is unprepared in experience or facilities. The architect's overall knowledge of the building industry makes it possible for him to advise the client as to the most effective matching of the contractor's capabilities to the project in question. Then, too, the client secures experienced counsel regarding his own rights and responsibilities, bonds and insurance, and the relationships of the various parties to the contract.

In certain cases the congregation may prefer to enter into separate contracts for different parts of the construction work, and retain the architect to coordinate them. Under such arrangements the detailed knowledge of the architect with respect to the special trades is of inestimable value.

E. The Construction Stage

After the signing of the construction contract and during construction, the architect performs for the client eight types of services: a. investigation and approval of subcontractors; b. preparation of required large-scale and full-size details; c. approval of materials, equipment, finishes, and other matters; d. checking of shop drawings; e. periodical review of the work to assure reasonable compliance to drawings and specifications; f. certification of requisition for payments; g. negotiation of changes in the contract; h. final inspection and certification of the completed project.

In certain types of projects, large details are included in the working drawings but normally they are reserved for the construction stage. All other services during construction are performed, however,

as the client's agent, for his protection, as well as to facilitate the smooth progress and satisfactory completion of the project. Although acting as the client's adviser, the architect is, at the same time, obligated to promote in every reasonable way the equitable operation of the contract.

By inspecting materials, equipment, finishes, color schedules, and the like, by checking the shop drawings prepared by fabricators, and by supervising actual construction and the installation of equipment, the architect, although he cannot guarantee the contractor's work, goes far to assure the owner that it conforms to that called for by the contract documents. If continuous inspection at the site is necessary, as is often the case on large projects, the client can provide a full-time inspector, at owner's expense, who then serves under the approval and direction of the architect. In most cases, however, if the contractor has been selected wisely and if the project is not too large or complex, the architect's visits to the site as needed in the work will be sufficient. In all these services, the architect, through his technical knowledge and skill and his detailed familiarity with the specific project, contributes to the progress of the work by forestalling misunderstandings, arbitrating disputes, apprehending errors and directing their correction.

The last three services — the certification of payments, negotiation of contract changes, and final review — are administrative functions which help to maintain smooth operation of the contract.

The architectural services described are used today for all projects designed by architects. The pattern of these services is the result of long development by the profession in an effort to provide the most effective and equitable method possible by which clients and society can procure maximum value.

Engaging an architect is the same as retaining a lawyer or selecting a doctor. Training and ability are important — worth considering, too, is personality, as the client is going to spend a great deal of time with his architect. The following methods of procedure for the selection of an architect are customary:

DIRECT SELECTION. Selection by the owner through personal knowledge on the basis of reputation, demonstrated ability, and the recommendations of others for whom the architect has rendered his service.

COMPARATIVE SELECTION. Selection from a group of architects given opportunity to present evidence of their qualifications, the owner acting with or without the advice of an architect serving as a professional adviser.

DESIGN COMPETITION SELECTION. Selection according to Architectural Competition Code Procedure of the American Institute of Architects. (Information on the procedure may be had by writing AIA headquarters in Washington, D. C.) Cost of competition shall be borne by the owner. It can be a very expensive method.

As in any other profession, fees for architectural services vary, and depend on an architect's standing in his field, geographic location of office, size and kind of job to be done, and his estimation of his own competence and qualification.

The architect, in accord with his code of ethics, does not accept discounts or commissions; his only remuneration is that received from his client.

The architect's fee is settled at an early conference with final arrangements stated in a formal contract or by letter, countersigned by congregation and architect.

The fee varies with individual cases, depending on the amount of services required. The contract may provide for a consultation for architectural advice on buying and remodeling an old church or on the selection of a lot and complete architectural services to be rendered from beginning to end.

Some of the finest examples of church and church school architecture have been designed by architects doing their first job in this field. Many architects who engage in a well-diversified practice have a broader approach to a given problem than those working within a restricted practice and are, therefore, worthy of consideration for selection.

The picture of the architect painted in this chapter stresses training and competence which can cope with the multitude of complex problems that face churches of all denominations in developing their building programs and producing honest, lasting architecture expressive of the times and fostering the spiritual and religious rebirth essential to the permanence of the church.

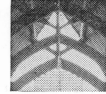

Chapter 5

MASTER PLANNING

As the United States changed from a predominately rural nation to a series of large and small urban complexes brought about by the worldwide industrial revolution, it became increasingly apparent that some kind of control must be exercised through plans — long-range plans, master plans — to cope with this development.

The industrialization of the United States, the use of all kinds of motor vehicles, the construction of highway systems, the commerical use of the airplane, the speed of transportation, mass communication media, more speed, then the atom and the jet age — all of these have been compressed into a relatively short space of history — some 50 years — the span of two generations. The results brought mass shifts in population, increase in population, new cities, growing cities, and at the same time decaying cities, economic shifts and changes, and in many cases utter chaos. Overburdened city governments, overburdened state governments, exploding population of school districts, inflation, more taxes followed.

This is pertinent to the subject of master planning of churches. Churches are an integral part of all community life, rural and urban, and all of the changes in the past 50 years have affected the planning, location, design, and general pattern of today's church.

In retrospect one can be critical of the church fathers of two generations past on the basis of lack of foresight in purchasing church sites of inadequate size and improper location and for not anticipating some of the mid-20th-century phenomena of growth. To be critical is unfair and unwarranted, as prac-

tically no area of business, government, education, or the church remotely anticipated the impact of the automobile, the airplane, the vacuum tube, or the atom. The world has not been able to change human nature since the dawn of civilization, but the set of rules and conditions that govern and control human conduct has changed drastically so that the program of procedure is a new one with many additional features not dreamed about 50 years ago except by H. G. Wells, Jules Verne, and other imaginative writers.

Therefore communities large and small have prepared master plans of broad import, with police power sanctioned by the courts, to cope with existing physical conditions and to anticipate future trends and growth. Thus it is toward a double-barreled objective that the master plan of the community is directed, forestalling the drift into chaos in the yet undeveloped areas of the city and promoting the gradual reconstruction of the developed area of the city, with particular attention to blighted sections and improved circulation of traffic. The present chaotic development of the community or city is a trend which may be corrected and redirected when the advantages of planning are appropriately exploited.

The master plan appraises the changing nature of the community and defines its natural character. It evaluates trends in the local urban economy and analyzes services and functions. It requires adjustments in the living habits of the people, land use, and transportation, to insure a favorable environment in which to live and work. The master plan sets forth adjustments graphically and thereby becomes a guide for the future growth and development of the community. It reflects a knowledge of the physical structure of the community, of natural uses of the land, and of existing functions; these things merit recognition and respect in the plan.

The master plan also recognizes the links with neighboring communities — cities and towns — and environs by means of the highways, railroads, airports, and mass transportation facilities. It reflects policies as to the density of population desirable and consistent with the character of the community in its residential areas. Furthermore it indicates the standards for the relation of building bulk and open space in these areas, and also in commercial, industrial, and multiple-family areas. The broad land use plan is guided by these standards, and the precise plans for the various areas of the city are refined. Schools, playgrounds, parks, churches, neighborhood units, local shopping centers, freeways, rapid-transit arteries are all considered in proper relationships to the residential, commercial, "downtown" business center, and industrial areas. Such master planning sets forth the appropriate use to which the land in the community may be devoted so that the enterprise of community building may have a tangible guide in its determinations of investment. Thus zoning is a facet of the master plan and is one of the tools used to implement its broad aspects.

One can readily see that the church is subject to the objectives of the area master plan and in its own master planning must conform to the restrictions that protect the value and stability of its property and physical development, present and future. It is good stewardship for the church body to appreciate the value and protection that a master plan affords it in the community and, in turn, to develop a master plan of its own property, based on the same governing principles that direct the community planning process.

Many painful examples of lack of stewardship on the part of old and new church congregations can be cited where master plans were not prepared and the costly results of such shortsightedness have run into hundreds of thousands of dollars of waste, in many cases resulting in the failure of new mission church congregations, since the growth pattern was so rapid that the choice of site, the size of the building, and the plan layout of the first unit were not made with sufficient foresight in the initial stage. Church master planning requires vision and imagination.

It is a simple matter to obtain a copy of the local master plan and zoning requirements, which will embrace the following important information, all vital to the future congregational welfare:

1. Land use designations for the area in which the church is located and in which its members live.
2. A forecast of population trends.
3. Zoning restrictions and their effect on planning of the church property, with particular reference to off-street parking requirements.
4. Availability of transportation, present and future.
5. The major highway pattern for the community and how it affects the church site.
6. Future overall prospects for the community, region, state, or geographical section of the country.
7. How much of the "fluid process" or inherent provision for change is apparent in the master plan as it might affect the church.

All of the above information can be evaluated as it influences the existing church. In some cases it may even determine whether a second look should be taken as to the adequacy of the present site. In the case of a new congregation, extensive investigation based on the above should be made prior to selecting a location for a new church, and it is strongly recommended in this instance that an architect be engaged for the program to assist and advise in the site selection. Site selection is covered in another chapter of this book and is only touched on here to indicate its importance in the overall picture.

The master plan and its requirements should be established by the planning committee in its development of a comprehensive building program. Recognizing that each congregation has a personality of its own and that its detailed requirements are also distinct, the master plan should take this into account in its formulation. Thus the master plan becomes an important function of the planning committee, which determines the elements to be included after all of the church's vital statistics have been recorded.

The requirements of one Protestant church group in the establishing of new congregations are a good example of a realistic and intelligent approach to good stewardship in building construction. Before church funds are made available for construction they require:

1. The selection of an adequate site within the

framework of a realistic budget and the community's master plan.

2. The appointing of a planning committee.
3. The development of a building program based on the congregation's vital statistics.
4. The appointing of a building committee.
5. The selection of an architect.
6. The developing of the master plan at a legible scale by the architect in such detail as to show all survey information covering site boundaries, present contours, all streets, easements, setback lines, utilities, and major trees to be preserved. The overall ultimate building plan is shown with all areas assigned, floor elevations established, finished grades marked, and all site improvements such as walks, drives, access ways, and parking indicated. Then another drawing is made onto the same scale showing the "initial building plan" and additional information covering the immediate stage and the limited site improvement work in this phase of the budget.

With these established drawings of the ultimate and initial portions of the master plan, the congregation has a guide for approximately 20 years, with any or all of it to be completed as growth demands and the funds become available. It is spared the frustration and embarrassment of having the first stage of construction improperly placed on the building site to the detriment of future development.

The master plan to a degree is a fluid process in the sense that certain changes may become apparent during the years that may modify or alter elements in the plan as originally developed. This fluid process does not imply that decisions are not represented in the ultimate master plan, but that all such plans recognize changes that are inherent, whether they be made for an individual project or for an entire city or region.

Congregations would do well to avoid the preparation of merely a pretty picture of an overall so-called master plan that does not include serious study and ultimate preparation of realistic factual drawings that establish location of all elements in the plan. Normally the preparation of such drawings for a master plan is recognized as additional work on the part of the architect, and therefore additional compensation is made for this service.

As the master plan for a city is a design for the physical, social, economic, and political framework of the city, which welds the sociological, economic, and geographic properties of the city into a structure, so the master plan of a church recognizes the church's personality, evaluates its vital statistics and activity needs, programs current and future development, establishes physical elements in a plan of successive construction stages. Above all such a master plan expresses the aspirations and philosophy of the church in a set of ideals that will influence future decisions made within the framework of the master plan.

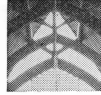

Chapter 6

THE PARISH SITE

The selection of a site for the church plant usually determines its long-range success and the future growth of the parish.

The expanding program of the Christian church precludes the selection of land purely on the basis of expediency or immediate availability.

Parish objectives, community development, population trends, and immediate physical site features all call for long-range evaluation on the part of the church's governing body, local, district, and regional, in collaboration with technical and professional advisers.

In the past it was intended that a parish serve its area for a minimum of 50 years. There are many instances, particularly in smaller eastern communities, where the original parish still thrives after several hundred years of service in its original location. Such uninterrupted service is found generally in municipalities of slow growth, unchanging land use, and slight ethnic change.

Competent and thorough study of community and regional characteristics and trends before the purchase of new parish sites becomes essential in this era of rapid growth and sudden change.

It is seldom possible to acquire a site which is ideal in all respects and still obtainable within the normal parish budget. Furthermore, there is an actual scarcity of land suitable for parish development within or near developed areas.

Nevertheless, it is essential that church plant requirements be established prior to site determination. This entails the projection of parish needs and scope into the future. The matter of multiple services, Christian day school expectancy, facilities for parking, recreation, and other functional factors all contribute to the ultimate size of the building complex and influence the eventual area of the building site.

Master planning at this early stage can be performed only upon a schematic basis, but if intelligently and imaginatively handled it can guide the congregation away from the more obvious pitfalls.

There is no greater frustration for the thriving congregation than to have its ambitions for expansion thwarted by irrevocable lot and boundary limitations or to find itself surrounded by mushrooming growth incompatible with its spiritual existence.

Conceding the inconvenience of entering into permanent architectural commitments so early in the program, it is nevertheless desirable to obtain some professional guidance during the preplanning period. Community development and environment, building codes and zoning, transportation and parking, subsurface investigation and topography, utilities and accessibility are matters closely identified with planning. Intelligent architectural advice at this stage will more than pay for itself in planning freedom for the future.

Site selection for the parish should pretend neither to be a mysterious art nor the exclusive domain of a particular profession. It should be considered in the light of sound business standards and established criteria. The church lives side by side with a culture afflicted with materialism. To the extent that this materialism does not impinge upon spiritual values there is much that the congregation can learn from it.

The accepted criteria of good business practice in selection of sites for commercial purposes can be applied also for parish purposes in the following particulars:

1. People (population)
2. Government (the community and environment)
3. Neighborhood and environment
4. Size of site (adequacy for present use and future expansion)
5. Traffic, transportation, and parking
6. Recreation
7. Accessibility
8. Utility services
9. Subsurface conditions and geology
10. Topography
11. Zoning and city planning regulations
12. Building code and municipal regulations
13. Adverse influences
14. Cost
15. Aesthetic factors

1. People (Population)

Each site under consideration must be related first to the individuals to which it will minister. If the site lies in a developed area, it is possible to arrive at conclusions based on past local experience. Census results and local planning statistics combined with the records of the religious district office are an obvious source of reliable information.

If a proposed site lies within the general boundaries of the established parish, then a great deal of data should be immediately available in the church records. The wall map with colored dots is an old established device which gives the comprehensive story at a glance.

Where a site is proposed in a completely new area outside the boundaries of the established parish and perhaps outside the fringe of an incorporated municipality, the evaluation of population expectancy becomes much more complex. Here no statistical stone should be left unturned. There may be many available.

Since the end of World War II the entire nation has been on a statistical forecasting spree. The population explosion, the decentralization of towns and cities, and the sudden mobility of our people have stimulated government and industry at all levels to study and forecast population and community trends.

Federal, state, and municipal agencies, regional and local planning bodies, both public and private, utility companies, educational boards, and college departments have developed survey upon survey, many quite up-to-date, reliable, and available for the asking.

The church should use every tool at hand to implement its decisions. Although much governmental planning has been derided as being irrelevant and inconsequential, there still remains a good hard core of valuable information for the church parish.

The available data should be studied carefully, the extraneous separated from the useful, and the remainder applied to the general pool of material required for intelligent site selection.

Currently there is a distressing delusion that the population of the American city is shrinking, and this has been used as a justification for the direction of mission efforts toward the suburbs. No one can deny the explosive impact of modern suburban growth. But it is erroneous to assume that our cities are becoming depopulated. We are essentially an urban society. Present city growth has flattened out or become static. But one fact remains: millions upon millions of our people still rely on the city for shelter and livelihood. The city congregation with suburban wanderlust should scrutinize its immediate forest before climbing the nearest tree for a look at the horizon.

Parish planning is not solely a matter of pencil lines on paper. That important phase should be preceded by business, social, and spiritual planning.

2. Government (the Community)

No parish can be an island by itself. For better or for worse it must maintain rapport with the municipality in which it lies. This consideration does not imply involvement in politics but rather a continuing awareness of what is going on.

Zoning laws and building codes are changed frequently; new planning agencies are disposed to revolutionary new concepts.

While the church in its interest in the community

should not necessarily oppose new legislative frontiers, it should be in a position to protect its interests when they are jeopardized. This is particularly applicable to the parish site, which is subject to all of the vagaries peculiar to other municipal real estate.

In each congregation there is usually at least one member who maintains entente with the overall community scene — a governmental employee, a realtor, an architect, an engineer, an attorney, or someone else. Such a person if properly authorized can be of indispensable value as a reporter to the church governing body.

Expressways and thruways are projected many years ahead. They have a tendency to isolate large areas from the stream of municipal life. Obviously, a site located within such an area would be of no use, no matter how low the land cost.

Inquiries at governmental sources from church groups are generally given special consideration. Career employees in government are usually familiar with long-range community objectives and willing to discuss their implications with persons officially representing church groups.

3. Neighborhood and Environment

High speed transportation and modern pace have removed the connotation that a neighborhood is where people live in fairly close proximity and in a general realm of friendliness. In the larger cities this definition applied only where people of similar ethnic and religious backgrounds grouped together in some form of residential harmony.

For a church, however, the original concept is still an important ideal. In its site selection, the religious and ethnic makeup of the neighborhood should be given maximum consideration. Mutual friendliness and helpfulness are of great value. This applies to the parish as a neighbor as well as to the surrounding residents. A church which purchases a site too small and overloads it with a multitude of facilities, followed by continuous day-in day-out social activity which spills over onto the neighbors' property in the form of illegal parking, congregating on sidewalks in the vicinity, noise and disturbance

late at night, can justly be categorized as an undesirable neighbor.

It is highly significant that in many parts of the country residential areas are restricted as to church use unless a variance is granted by the local zoning appeals board. This unusual situation is the outgrowth of an abuse of privilege by church bodies who refuse to recognize that tax-exempt use of land carries with it the duty of extending neighborly courtesy to the immediate community.

Conversely the committee on site selection should be careful to observe that the present neighborhood does not support influences harmful to continued parish development over a long period of years. Such factors will be more fully discussed.

4. Size of Site

In addition to the provision of adequate worship facilities the membership at large is looking to the church to provide educational, recreational, and social amenities. Such a comprehensive program, combined with attendant automobile parking, obviously cannot be accommodated on a quarter-acre plot.

Prior to the purchase of the site a well-conceived preliminary program combined with sound architectural advice can protect the parish from the most serious mistake of all in site choices — a plot too small. An experienced architect, referring to the program, can by rule of thumb establish building areas with reasonable accuracy for church, school, parish building, and recreation. Setback and area requirements of local zoning must be added to this total.

Ample provision for expandability involves a great degree of prayerful foresight. It is an important factor. Actually for the dynamic church no site can be too large. The outreach of Christianity is enormous. It should not be confined by niggardly land area.

If vacant land is limited, then the probability of future acquisition of adjacent improved properties should be investigated. The purchase of strategic locations can often be achieved where a congregation maintains good public relations with the local neighborhood.

5. Traffic, Transportation, and Parking

It is one of the great ironies that Christianity, which for some 1,900 years depended on the consecrated efforts of dedicated pedestrians, has now been taken over almost completely by the automobile.

Christ walked quietly but significantly along the paths and lakefront of a very modest part of the earth. His apostles and the saints strode with giant steps to the far corners of the earth and for almost 20 centuries people tried to walk in Christ's footsteps to their places of worship. Medieval pilgrimages and the crusades were made largely by people on foot. There were few vehicles, fewer roads, and traffic problems, where they existed, went unrecognized.

With the 20th century came the automobile — and with it a revolutionary change in all aspects of living and an abundance of problems in American community, industrial, and religious life.

He who aspires to choose a parish site without considering the influence of the automobile is either a man of infinite faith or a great fool. Traffic jams, transportation bottlenecks, and parking inadequacies, along with air pollution, highway accidents, death tolls, and teen-age immorality are the by-products of the great automotive age. Traffic could be defined as a many-celled serpent with no head, no tail, and no objective. It can be totally destructive to a parish site. Its side effects should not be underestimated.

A 60-mile-an-hour freeway is certainly carrying no parishioners to church. The same applies to the arterial highway which connects city to suburb. Sites in the proximity of such routes should be avoided, since they bisect and isolate communities and neighborhoods as would a nerve operation.

Similarly, local roads which are heavily traveled should be avoided as boundary streets unless the site is large and adequately served by secondary roads and protected by broad buffer strips.

The difficulty of making left turns off main routes is recognized by local authorities, but traffic control agencies are often overzealous in their control efforts. A church site exposed to left-hand-turn restrictions, heavy traffic concentrations, one way streets, and long-interval traffic lights has a built-in disadvantage.

The avoidance of heavily traveled roads does not imply that the selected church site should be tucked away on a quiet country road. Ideally it should be located on well-traveled roads in good condition with a minimum of through traffic. To some extent heavy traffic and good transportation go hand in hand. Therefore it is difficult to avoid some adverse traffic conditions.

Each prospective site should be carefully related to the nearest bus station, bus stops, and taxi stands. The great mobility of the American public makes it possible to develop accessible outlying sites. Notwithstanding this, it must be borne in mind that not every family uses two cars, nor does each individual have such transportation at his disposal at all times. Conceding that walking to church is an anachronism, it does not follow that everyone must travel by automobile. Since, however, most churchgoers rely on the family car, we are led directly into the next problem of our age, the question of parking.

Probably the most irritating neighborhood factor arises when parish activities are of such a nature that parking spills out along the curb perimeter for several blocks in all directions. When an unbeliever on his way to the beach on Sunday morning finds his driveway blocked by the car of a churchgoer, such a situation does little to raise the stature of churchgoers or improve the disposition of the unbeliever.

There is a very strong trend today to require all church parking to take place within the church site. In extreme cases this can compel the parish to create colossal parking areas on the basis of one car for each two pew seats. The arithmetical implications of this formula are somewhat absurd. The nave of a church can accommodate approximately one person for each eight gross square feet. To park an automobile on site requires approximately 250 to 300 square feet gross for each parked car.

High-percentage parking is an obvious impossibility in the instance of most parishes, particularly those of urban or even suburban areas. Such a requirement is most serious, however, in that it narrows down substantially the number of eligible sites. Combined with this problem, which is both economic and physical, there is the congestion and confusion which arises where services are held on an end-to-end basis. To empty a parking area while other cars are entering presents almost impossible complications.

There are numerous examples of churches which have sites located adjacent to shopping centers and have made successful use of the sizable parking areas essential to these commercial uses. If such an arrangement is possible without seriously compromising other site criteria, it should receive full consideration. The presence of the church in the marketplace is not an incongruity.

6. Recreation

The church community is not complete without space for outdoor and indoor recreation. Obviously this cannot always be provided. Initial cost factors and maintenance responsibilities can be prohibitive. Tennis, softball, or basketball courts all require sizable lot areas, and very often facilities for these activities are offered through the municipality.

Some recreational space should be available on the parish site. A Christian day school without appropriate recess area is seriously restraining its pupils during the long school day and placing a difficult supervisory responsibility on the faculty. A moderate amount of supervised physical activity during school hours develops a more tractable and cooperative child and a less harassed faculty.

Intelligent location and treatment of the parking area will permit it to be used as a recreational area during nonworship hours.

A small, permanently equipped playground solely for use by preschool and kindergarten children can be of inestimable value.

7. Accessibility

The sentimental exclusiveness of the quiet church in the forest glen is not without its nostalgic appeal. The well-worn path attests to the fact that people will seek out the church.

But we live in a materialistic age in which undue emphasis is placed on convenience and creature comforts. To offset the many distractions of modern culture, the church must seek out the people. This can be best accomplished through the selection of a dynamic location which emphasizes prominence and accessibility.

No modern commercial location is acquired without positive assurance that the people constituting the market will have direct access to it. A church should have similar contiguity to the souls it serves.

8. Utility Services

Virtually all established incorporated municipal areas throughout the country are reasonably well equipped with the normal utility services: sewers, water, electricity, and gas.

Newer mushrooming suburban areas have been hard pressed to keep abreast of the ever-increasing demand for services for residential and commercial use.

Where adequate normal public services are available, a congregation is well advised to connect to these in preference to developing local on-site services. Driven wells and private disposal systems require maintenance and possess the perverse habit of failing at inopportune times. In some districts the level of the water table has dropped alarmingly due to greatly increased use of well water.

The architectural adviser can assist the congregation in securing information from the local public works office and public utility companies. A memorandum and diagram showing the size and location of the various services should be filed for future reference purposes.

9. Subsurface Conditions and Geology

Biblical references to the need for a firm foundation and solid subsurface have gone unheeded all too often for buildings of all types.

In areas where there is a regional geological uniformity a certain amount of assumption or deduction is permissible; but wherever even a slight geologic capriciousness is suspected, subsurface exploration and soil analysis are an absolute requirement before site acquisition. Acceptability of the subsurface should be made a condition of the land purchase contract.

Many sites have notably met all of the apparent criteria but have cost their new owner a totally disproportionate sum because of extraordinary foundation conditions. No building scheduled to cost $100,000 can afford to stand on a $200,000 foundation.

Test pits, core or wash borings under the scrutiny of a competent soils analyst can supply information leading to the purchase or rejection of a doubtful site and can be invaluable to the architect during the siting or planning of the structure.

10. Topography

The congregational building committee is now entering deeper waters and will find much greater buoyancy if it leans more heavily on its technical advisers for guidance. Contrary to popular impression, flat or dead-level sites are by no means the best parish sites. Sloping or rolling sites are easier to drain, offer easier landscaping opportunities, and permit better natural lighting of basement spaces if these are properly disposed.

But it does not follow that all hilly sites are preferable. Automobiles are difficult to park on sloping areas, and excessive steps between different levels are inconvenient, particularly for older parishioners. It is essential that if the proposed land presents uphill or reverse-slope problems it receive preliminary scrutiny by an architect.

11. Zoning and City Planning Regulations

Generations of abuse and misuse of land have brought about the enactment of stringent zoning laws and the strengthening of the jurisdiction of local planning boards.

No parish site should be acquired without an exhaustive study of current and projected zoning and planning legislation. In the instance of smaller plots in highly restrictive areas zoning laws may be confiscatory; administration by the local board, arbitrary.

No property owner or real estate man can guarantee the granting of a variance before a hearing has been held; neither can a congregation assume that it will receive preferred consideration because of its religious status. Highly restricted communities are often opposed to the exception and assessment benefits normally extended to church bodies and therefore disinclined to concede variance requests.

Land which carries a price tag per acre of $10,000 may be reasonable in cost until one evaluates the land loss incurred by 25-percent coverage limitations, 100-foot main street setback requirements and 50-foot side and rear line setbacks, combined with confiscatory on-site parking requirements. These factors should all be known beforehand; if variances are required, the approval of these should be conditional to the contract of sale of the land.

12. Building Codes and Municipal Regulations

Uniformity of building regulations is a worthy objective which falls far short of fulfillment. Contiguous communities may have individual building codes completely unrelated to each other in approach, scope, or cost implications. Where one of these communities insists on totally fireproof construction for churches while the other allows conventional construction, there the building cost differential is properly chargeable as a function of land cost because it occurs only by virtue of the geographical location of the proposed building.

Building regulation is a highly uneven part of American local government. It is unpredictable, inconsistent, and dangerously variable. It is sensitive to spectacular news stories of building failures and fires involving loss of life. For instance, the tragic Chicago parochial school fire will have repercussions for years to come. It has already introduced a system of fire department review which actually duplicates or supersedes building department jurisdiction.

In this connection the parish should guard itself against unreasonable and excessive local building regulation. Obviously, exit facilities should be adequate and conveniently located, but there is no justifiable reason why a church or parish school should be built like Fort Knox.

Here the architect can advise and counsel because of his familiarity with local practice, combined with his ability to consult and negotiate with proper officials.

13. Adverse Influences

Exploration of the adverse influences at a specific site is as important before its acquisition as is a full realization of its advantages. It may, for instance, be near a source of noise, smoke, dust, or noxious odors. There may be outside distractions which will take attention away from services. Airfields nearby, traffic hazards, and inaccessibility too must be considered adverse influences.

Very few sites approach perfection. A certain degree of adversity is inherent in every human transaction, but it is much better to possess an awareness of this prior to rather than after acquisition.

An option to purchase land after the expiration

of a stipulated period is normal to most land transactions. The option period should be utilized to balance site advantages against disadvantages. It is generally not too difficult to judge which side of the balance carries the greater weight.

14. Cost

After years of blundering timidity in site selection, churches of all denominations have come to realize that the cheapest land can be, in the long run, the most expensive. Poor subsurfaces, confiscatory building regulations, lack of suitable public services, and declining community social trends combine to depress land value or raise the cost of construction.

Consequently there is no rule of thumb which can be applied to all sites in a given community or all communities in a given state.

Land is particularly sensitive to inflationary impulses and speculative manipulation. It is therefore impossible for the average congregation to bid against commercial interests competing for a given site, particularly where tax exemption factors are involved.

15. Aesthetic Factors

The value of a fine aesthetic site background cannot be overestimated. A prominent location, good mature trees, parklike surroundings, or the proximity of a monumental setting all contribute to the beauty of a location.

Such situations are rare and add substantially to site value. Where conditions of this kind obtain, they present to the church architect a challenge to design a building which measures up to its surroundings.

There is probably no public relations factor equal to spontaneous public acceptance of a local building as a beautiful monument. To design and build a house of God is by its nature a presumptive act of man. But with prayer and spiritual inspiration a beautiful function can be accorded its proper dignity in its proper setting on God's earth.

Chapter 7

THE CHURCH PLAN

Man was created to worship God!

This is indicated in the first sacrifice of Abel, who in a true spirit of worship brought a thankoffering to the Lord. It is told in Gen. 8:20 that when Noah left the ark, he built an altar on which he offered burnt offerings to the Lord in thankfulness for his deliverance.

Jacob, after the vision of the ladder to heaven, said "and this stone which I have set for a pillar shall be God's house."

The Old Testament tells us that Moses, after the Amalekites were defeated in battle, built an altar and called the name of it "Jehovah Nissi" (Jehovah is my Banner). In Ex. 30 reference is made to the altar on which incense was to be burned.

In Ex. 25, 26, and 27 the Lord God instructed Moses as to the construction of the ark and the tabernacle. The specifications called for the most durable and costliest materials. Even though the children of Israel were wandering in the desert, the ark and the tabernacle were to be of these precious materials and finest fabrics. The curtains and coverings were not only rugged and durable, but were also of brilliant colors, "of blue and purple and scarlet, and fine twined linen wrought with needlework."

The importance of worship is also clearly indicated in Ex. 31, where we learn that the Lord reconsecrated the Sabbath which He had set apart at the time of creation.

While the children of Israel, due to their rebellious spirit, were doomed to wandering in the desert, once settled in the Land of Palestine the climax of their worshipful surroundings came in the grandeur of the temple of Solomon. This temple, which David was not privileged to build because of the wars he was forced to fight, was of the finest materials. It is an example of the earliest type of prefabrication. 1 Kings 6 and 7, the great construction chapters of the Old Testament, give a minute description of this wonderful edifice. That most of the temple was prefabricated is indicated in 1 Kings 6:7 where it states: "when it was in building, it was built of stone made ready before it was brought thither, so that there was neither hammer nor ax nor any tool of iron heard in the house while it was in building." Today we hear of modular construction, which means identical units of materials or multiple units which will equal certain overall measurements. Here is a very early indication of modular construction. 1 Kings 6:3 describes the sizes in "cubits." This varied with the length of the superintendent's or chief architect's or builder's forearm from the knuckle edge of the closed fist to the edge of the elbow and varied from 16 to 18 inches, depending on the size of the man in charge, or that of the master builder.

At the dedication of the temple, Solomon asked "But will God indeed dwell on the earth? Behold the heaven and heaven of heavens cannot contain Thee; how much less this house that I have builded?" Nevertheless the temple had been built at God's command.

The psalmist declares, "How amiable are thy tabernacles, O Lord of hosts."

Thus we see from these fragmentary quotations of

the Scriptures that the Lord does wish an earthly evidence of His presence, a place of worship.

In the New Testament our Lord Jesus Christ said: "Where two or three are gathered together in My name, there am I in the midst of them." It must be remembered that the God preached by St. Paul was not "like unto gold or silver, or stone, graven by art and man's device." The purpose of the early Christian church was to shelter the worshipers who met for prayer and praise of God. During the unsettled and turbulent times of the early New Testament era, various places were adapted for worship.

The early Christians thus met together first in their homes and synagogs and then, as persecution gained momentum, in secret places and catacombs. They were persecuted horribly and with systematic Roman vigor. It was not until the edict of Constantine in A. D. 313 that Christianity was officially accepted. As Christianity flourished, the buildings increased in size and significance.

There is strong evidence to indicate that even before the edict of Constantine Christian worship was practiced openly and above ground at various locations within the empire. It follows that such worship may have been practiced in the Roman basilica, used for tribunals and as a place of exchange or assembly.

The plan of the basilica consisted of a large open nave for public gatherings with a raised platform at one end and an entrance space or atrium at the portal. It was a natural setting for Christian worship and the development of basic Christian liturgy.

Buildings in the 4th to 7th centuries were developed from the Roman basilica tradition. As the early Christians were not wealthy, it was natural that they used, as far as possible, the materials from Roman temples which had become useless for their original purpose.

In this way the first buildings used as churches came into being. The early Christian churches were of the "Romanesque" or classic style. This permitted free use of the arch, vault, and dome, three basic forms of Roman architecture.

During the 12th through the 16th centuries the church gradually suffered an eclipse of power. In this Dark Age period, however, the seat of learning and of art and architecture remained with the ecclesiastics. As a protection against fire and invasion, natural architecture of stone developed. Artisans and artists from distant areas flocked to the communities where great cathedrals were being constructed. The imprint of their inner feelings and dedication re-

mains in the beautiful carvings and architectural effects of the Gothic cathedrals we know today. The classicists of the Romanesque period could not tolerate the buildings which contained none of the refined details of the former churches. The Goths were considered crude and barbaric people. Thus Gothic was the epithet of ridicule applied to this upstart in the construction techniques of that day. As today, new ideas were greeted with suspicion and derision.

However, the finest hour of church architecture to that time had been reached. The beautiful, honest buildings of the old world in the Gothic tradition bear proof of this.

The period of development of worship in the churches, from the earliest altars, gradually brought about greater and greater distances between clergy and laity. This was reflected in the plans of the churches as they were built. The laity was constantly pushed farther away from actual participation in the worship service. The Communion rail became a division between the worshiper and the chancel and sanctuary in which the altar was placed. More and more the worshiper followed the service or Mass by sounds, gestures, and genuflections. The services were learned by rote, and the people were exposed to images and religious formalism to fill their spiritual needs.

During the 16th-century Reformation, congregational participation gradually increased. The Reformation was not intended as a destruction of the Catholic religion but as a correction of the abuses which had infiltrated the whole fabric of Christian doctrine and worship.

The plans of the early Reformed churches were thus necessarily similar to the old tradition. True, more importance was attached to sermon than sacrament, and consequently images and artwork, which were deemed idolatrous, were often removed. In many instances, particularly in England, real art treasures were destroyed by overzealous reformists and vandals.

America was originally settled mostly by those seeking religious freedom: Pilgrims, Puritans, other Protestants, and Catholics, who settled along the Eastern Seaboard. Today the simple colonial churches of those days still dot the landscape. The church or meeting house was the center of the village. Usually located on the village green, it was the focal point of social and governmental functions as well as of religious worship.

In the southern areas and on the West Coast, from

Mexico City north, the Spanish brought the Catholic banner to our shores. In the West the simple Spanish mission, built of native materials, influenced the church design for many generations after the area came under American authority.

As the country grew, immigrants brought to all areas of our land their religious beliefs and backgrounds. Large communities of Lutheran families also settled in different areas. Their church was the center of their life. A single church would serve a great number of persons, accommodations of 1,200 to 1,500 seats being not uncommon. Because of this large capacity fewer churches were required. Most of these houses of worship were patterned after European churches, and an attempt was frequently made to re-create the atmosphere of the home church. While most of the buildings were physically well built, the planning and appearance was, in most cases, less acceptable. Most were brick or frame imitations, so-called "carpenter Gothic." Honest use of available building material and honest expression of structure were seldom in evidence. However, by tradition or by habit they became beautiful in the minds of the older members, largely because of sentimental associations. Others, built well, with good detail and structurally sound, are still to be found in the so-called inner-city portions of most metropolitan areas.

By reason of rapid population growth and use of the automobile during the past generation, the churches, of necessity, have moved further and further from the center of the city into the suburban areas surrounding the metropolis.

This has affected the programing and planning of every congregation. To maintain a personal relationship between pastor and members of the parish, smaller membership per congregation now seems advisable. Therefore more churches of the 300—400 seating range are being planned in more locations.

Multiple services provide flexibility where sudden growth or local conditions tax the adequacy of the facilities.

Liturgical requirements, centered around the worship service, are being more carefully studied. A closer relationship between the congregation as members of the priesthood of believers and the pastor in his function of ministering the means of grace is necessary. This gathering of the people around the altar as a family of the Christian church is reflected in the architecture of recent years. The so-called "church in the round" is an indication of this trend. Locating the altar away from the sanctuary wall and making it free-standing indicates that it is not only symbolic of our Lord but is also the holy table around which the congregation may gather as partakers of the Lord's Supper.

No matter what the building form, we all turn to the Lord's altar as the center of worship. The church is the outward symbol of God's grace towards man.

Whatever plan or form is selected for a new church building, it must be functionally efficient and adapted to denominational liturgical requirements. The development of an architectural conversation piece with built-in problems does credit to no one and invites congregational tensions during the entire life of the structure.

The quiet dignity of Communion can be totally disrupted and services delayed if the entrance to and departure from the Communion rail are not planned for smooth circulation.

The location of choir and organ must be related intimately to all local liturgical customs and must be placed for convenient and friendly rapport between chancel and choir.

Comfort and convenience are not out of place in a house of worship. Good planning will limit the number of steps and stairs, even to the extent of providing ramps for access to large gathering places, locating toilets and coatrooms conveniently, and providing direct and comfortable access to all portions of the structure.

Where the worship areas become part of a large building complex, the sanctuary must be located in a position of complete privacy so that it cannot serve as a corridor, joining various areas of the development.

Good planning evolves from a well-drawn building program, developed through the cooperative effort of building committee and architect. No wholly successful building can be produced where interior plan and exterior elevation are not interrelated.

Man was created to worship God!

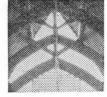

Chapter 8

THE FIRST UNIT

The three most exciting and provocative words in the history of mankind introduce the first line of Genesis — "In the beginning. . . ." No person, blessed with normal curiosity, can resist the invitation to pursue this introduction deeper and deeper into the core of the most significant and rewarding message written by God for the hearts of men.

The opening lines of a play, the initial chapter of a book, the first well-delivered lines of a speech or sermon establish the tone and pattern which command attention and develop coherence in literature, art, or achitecture. The human family attaches great, and sometimes excessive, importance to first things — the firstborn, a child's first steps, first in one's class, or first in social life or business. How often, however, is this devotion to beginnings set aside during the initial stages of the church building program!

This discussion would be superfluous were all parishes blessed with sufficient funds to attain their many-sided program objectives in one splendid, complex building operation — church, parsonage, parish hall, and school — all to the glory of God and the complacency of future generations of parishioners.

Fortunately for the continued vitality of the Kingdom, it is not ordained that all building problems are to be solved by a single gesture. Just as man's spiritual growth may develop over decades, so the complete fulfillment of the physical church plant may take several generations.

Therefore at an early stage the pastor and his congregation must decide what comes first. This is a vital decision which, if capriciously arrived at, could affect the future destiny of the parish.

The greater percentage of congregations embarking on building ventures in new locations usually find themselves short of funds but long on faith, inspiration, and dedication. And with these last three as assets, they are by no means impoverished, but prudence and Christian wisdom dictate the obligation to build in stages.

The cost of land and its attendant real estate and legal commitments, the cost of technical services, surveys, subsurface investigations, and other financial obligations often limit the congregation, in its initial phase, to a single unit of the ultimate building group.

But although the single unit may be modest in its general concept, it must be a vital and coordinated element of the master plan, elsewhere discussed. Just as no man can be an island to himself, neither can a building be less than a part of its own continent.

Where the first-unit approach is necessary, full realization of this requirement must be made known to the architect at the earliest stage. This will involve choice of whichever element of the building complex receives this primary designation, because it must contain the various mechanical services and it must be functionally adequate to serve the congregation during the early years.

This last factor involves most serious and prayerful consideration. During the early years of American religious life a church building was designed to satisfy the requirements of Sunday worship and little else. For the balance of the week the building remained an unused sanctuary, left vacant to usher in the beginning of another week. The problem of first-unit planning is peculiar to modern American culture.

Since the first quarter of the 20th century the limited scope of the sphere of the church has been broadened to embrace all aspects of Christian activity. Education, recreation, and Christian sociability and companionship are all considered as valid concerns by the church, for its people.

Which of these, then, is first in importance? The answer to this question is readily available and clear-cut — *worship!* But what about recreation, Christian companionship for our older people? More important, what about religious education for our children and, in fact, for the entire congregation? So our ready answer becomes clouded and complicated by the daily and, sometimes, mundane impact of modern life on the well-rounded church program.

All denominations and most congregations and families have developed an intelligent awareness of the need for meeting the religious and secular educational requirements of both child and adult. Whether this challenge is met in Sunday school or Christian day school or both, it requires the provision of adequate, well-planned space for such an activity.

To provide a place of worship alone, without facilities for children, deprives the church of the vigor and fertility of young families.

We have, then, the necessity of providing space which will, perhaps on a temporary basis, fulfill the requirements of worship and education without excessive compromise of either use.

Where funds are available, the solution to this problem can be oversimplified by simply referring to the master plan and erecting the complete worship and educational facilities, leaving for the future the development of the recreational and social facilities.

More often than not, funds are not available for such an ambitious inital effort. Were only the shell of the church itself erected in its entirety, it would involve considerations in layout and installed materials that could dissipate funds for the educational wing.

There are numerous successful examples where the church was limited to the erection of the chancel and several bays for worshipers, plus a partial educational wing. A departure from this arrangement would be found in the erection of the partial church as described previously, combined with a partial basement, available for Sunday school and other activities.

Basement space below churches has been the subject of time-honored discussion and debate. As a rule, unless there are favorable topographical conditions which raise a substantial portion of the space above grade, basements are not desirable.

On level sites where they are raised above grade for light and air, it follows that the church above must be raised above the grade level. This is aesthetically unpleasant and, even more important, requires long, tiresome stair runs between grade level and church floor — an extreme hardship to older people and a hazard to others at all times.

To depress the basement completely below grade gives rise to many other problems. Properly designed retaining walls are costly, as is the task of removing rock or earth from deep-cut excavations. Water and dampness are indigenous to cellars, and their presence makes such spaces functionally undesirable and unhealthful for children. Health authorities frown upon even the limited use of such space.

No discussion of cellar or basement church accommodations is complete without reference to the first-phase unit which is all basement or all cellar — a place for the worship of God underground, erected in the somewhat despairing hope that someday, somehow a church building will be superimposed on it. As a matter of semantic camouflage it is sometime designated as an undercroft, probably on a rationalization that if the early Christians could worship in the catacombs, so can we.

Of all the many available solutions to the problem of the first unit, the basement church is the one which combines the least faith with the greatest potential frustration. Let it be remembered that when Constantine made peace with the church in the 4th century, the Christians, as one man, emerged from their damp subterranean cellars and built permanent structures, beautiful in the sight of angels and men. The smallest church, standing proud and clean in God's sunlight, can bear witness just as man can.

We have discussed the feasibility of a combination first unit — part church, part school. Such initial disposition of space should adequately accommodate the worship requirements of the older parishioners and the educational needs — in part, at least — of children and young people. It would not fulfill the demand of recreational and social space.

In new and younger congregations, where there is an absence of pressure from older established congregational dynasty for a "complete" church building and nothing else, it may be desirable to consider a multipurpose parish hall and educational wing combination. Multipurpose is a much-abused phrase, which quite often describes a building facility which is all things to all people but satisfying to no one.

It is altogether inappropriate to use dedicated worship space for the usual social purposes, no matter how innocuous. The propriety of using a church nave for basketball or badminton need not even be considered. Far better would it be in most instances to contemplate a first-unit effort in terms of a combination parish hall and educational building. Where the new parish is completely new and not a congregation relocated because of condemnation for public improvement, this possibility should be thoroughly explored.

Young people with children, and those new in the church will more readily accept the idea of worship in a parish hall than older people who have a church tradition.

A parish hall, resourcefully designed for versatility of use, can offer a temporary, adequate setting for worship (the chancel can be screened off) and, in addition, answer virtually all of the social and recreational needs of the congregation. With realistic allowance for the fact that it does represent somewhat of a planning compromise, it offers greater opportunity for the many-sided program of the modern church, without limiting basic worship.

Objections previously raised to basements do not apply as strongly to the parish hall in that location, provided that good judgment is used in relating its floor level to the outside grade level. Similarly, the thought of a two-story relationship between parish hall and classrooms is not onerous if limited-site conditions favor an arrangement of this kind. In this connection, however, it should be remembered that excessively long stair runs impose physical strain on the aged and complicate control over youngsters. Ramps of moderate slope and length are preferable except in severe-weather areas.

The impact of climate on design is as pertinent for the first unit as it is for the entire religious complex. Winter severity may impose extreme hardship on a building improperly designed. The slab on the ground suited to a building in Ohio may be incompatible with the rigors of a Wisconsin winter or the permafrost of Canada.

Thus far we have considered three possibilities for the first unit: the church only, the church plus educational facilities, and the parish hall plus educational facilities. Two alternatives remain: the parish hall alone, and the church plus parish hall.

The church plus parish hall would provide for a congregation a workable unit, quite compatible with the many-sided activities of the modern parish. However, initial partial units must be committed to their ultimate use. If the completed parish hall envisions provisions for basketball and other athletic activities, its height and dimensions may involve costs not within the reach of the early program.

Construction of the parish hall alone entails operating difficulties almost insurmountable for the normally active congregation. In this day the doors of the church are always open. Many parish programs are conducted simultaneously, and these often run the full gamut of all age groups. To hold a teenage meeting and, perhaps, a weekday Bible study gathering in the same space with temporary dividers is to create a situation not favorable to the objectives of either group.

The advantage of conducting Sunday school simultaneously with, but in a different location from, one of the worship services is obvious, particularly where children are driven to the church site by their parents. Growth potential is greater where a new congregation offers these facilities, even on a modest initial scale.

It is not the intent of these pages to set forth a dogma which must be followed. Physical conditions will vary with each new congregation across the country. We do plead for intelligent and prayerful study, leading to the best possible relationship of the dynamic church program to its initial physical plant.

Whatever decision is eventually reached must bear direct relationship to the master plan. To develop a first unit without ultimate planning relationship is to risk waste of funds and misuse of land.

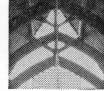

Chapter 9

THE CHURCH AND EDUCATION

Since the end of World War II an unprecedented volume of school construction has been matched by an accompanying mass of criticism and recrimination. Part of this has been directed toward modern progressive educational systems; other attacks have been leveled against the teaching profession; a great deal of public outcry has been directed toward alleged extravagances in design and construction.

To many Americans the one-room country schoolhouse is not just a nostalgic myth or legend. It represents an actual experience full of rich personal memories. Hence, public bewilderment and frustration over the modern abundance of luxurious facilities as opposed to the mediocre and restless student output are quite understandable.

Great physical beauty alone does not make a successful building. The architect must face the fact that just as a church building is incomplete without God and a home without love, so is a school building or system deficient without dedicated teaching and competent administration.

The great teachers of ancient times sat with their students in the open marketplace, and the schoolmen of the early middle ages carried on their work behind the grim walls of fortresslike castles and monasteries. In each case the school building as such took a secondary position to the quality of the teaching.

In our country, generations of Americans have received a fine and complete education in buildings of indifferent design and mediocre planning but with staffs of inspired individuals who regarded teaching as the highest profession.

The present American educational plant has been brought up to an unparalleled level physically, unequaled at any time or place in history. Many new school buildings are masterful in their planning and design; nearly all are equipped to the point of luxury.

The architect, however, with this beautiful plant, must realize that even with an unlimited budget the finest building alone will fall far short of the basic objective of training the child if the teaching is not commensurate.

Designing and planning for religious work are simplified to some extent by budgetary limitations. By a process of elimination the final planning complex is generally restricted to the fundamental areas of learning and recreation, with very little emphasis on nonessentials.

This fact places on the architect the combined privilege and responsibility of spending every educational building dollar with prayerful judgment. He will be unable to accomplish this without careful personal research into the educational requirements of each parish client. There are no consultants or experts available in the religious educational field, and the immediate experience in various areas of the country is either quite limited or totally lacking.

It is a fact generally overlooked that public education was uncommon in the United States until some years after the War of Independence. Many denominations carried on their state church traditions brought here from the old land in the field of education, and not without honor. The standard of literacy among the early leaders of the country remained at a high level well into the 19th century.

The English heritage of 18th-century eloquence remained with our forefathers and their children. For this we are indebted to education as promoted by the established churches of all denominations during the later Colonial and early Federal period.

And then the pendulum swung in the opposite direction, and generations of Americans were educated in the public realm. Their children forgot that church-sponsored education had ever existed, and their children's children, in their ignorance of the tradition, took the position that parish education was a new thing.

So today we stand in an era of confusion and lack of understanding which makes competitors of religiously and publicly sponsored educational groups.

Actually each has a great deal to learn from the other. The extreme materialism of public education has given the country many ceramic-lined swimming pools and an even greater number of vacuous minds. At the same time, parochial education has been too timid to participate in a franchise which it originally owned. The two groups, which normally socialize together, work together, and join in welfare endeavors, in the field of education regard each other with uncertainty and fail to cooperate.

It is at this point that the architect can render his greatest service. He can serve as a catalyst between the two groups, conveying to his religious client the wealth of data and information that has accrued in the field of building for public education over the past 15 or 20 years.

But before he can act in this capacity with any discernment, he must know his client and his immediate and future educational needs.

The scope of architecture today has broadened considerably and requires that the architect apply the modern techniques of research and market analysis before attempting to develop a solution to a building problem.

The research approach is particularly appropriate in planning for Christian education. In many areas of the country the idea of a parish school represents a dramatic departure from the established local pattern of public education. Therefore the architect, in close collaboration with his client, must approach his problem with carefully calculated steps, using the combined knowledge and experience of the local parish pastor, the district or regional advisory offices, and the educational facilities offered by the central religious body.

The steps involved in the study and development of a religious educational plant comprise the following:
1. Research (parish and district)
2. Programming (immediate and future)
3. Master planning
4. Preliminary planning
5. Site considerations
6. General considerations

1. Research

Time and energy spent in research and survey work during the early stages of planning a Christian day school will represent the difference between a carefully studied, successful solution and one which fails to meet educational needs.

It is a rare congregation which, when first embarking on a Christian day school venture, does not present divided opinions. Young married parishioners with children of preschool age are obviously more inclined to favor parish education than those whose children have completed their education. The financial impact of a school program on a parish can call for substantial sacrifice, and the older parishioners could understandably resist any change in the comfort and convenience of the status quo.

In this early analysis certain questions must be considered: Is a Christian day school justified for this particular parish? There could very well be a negative answer. Local public schools could be so conveniently placed and so well run that the church could supplement them through released time by building up its own religious program for school-age children. An adjacent parish may have developed, over the years, an efficient, well-staffed Christian day school of sufficient size and potential to serve the other neighboring congregations. Here we face the classic situation of congregational autonomy in relation to responsibility to the Kingdom at large. Paradoxically, the greatest strength and weakness in American Protestantism is bound up in the autonomy of the individual congregation. The weakness is emphasized if the thinking and decisions are made on a parochial basis. The strength develops when all parishes are guided to look to the general welfare, beyond local boundaries.

After the necessity for a local school has been decided, its size and scope remain to be established. Here the local pattern must be explored. Shall it be kindergarten—6, or kindergarten—8? The status of religious and public secondary schools should be the determining factor. To deviate from the local pattern is disturbing to parents and distracting to pupils. Children are not amenable to change.

How many grades in a classroom? The teacher shortage and local economies have obliged many religious day schools to operate with two grades in a single room. While this is considered substandard in public education, it is not uncommon in religious education. Here the ability of the teacher counts heavily; also the number of pupils per classroom is a factor. Kindergarten work should be confined to an individual classroom, and where funds and facilities permit, the first and eighth grades should be limited to single rooms to advantage. This would leave the second and third, fourth and fifth, sixth and seventh grades to be doubled up. For such an arrangement a six-classroom school would suffice. If the school principal teaches the eighth grade only, the children will be better prepared for high school and the principal will have more time available for his daily administrative functions.

Should there be a kindergarten? Heretofore established religious educational agencies have regarded kindergarten as a glorified form of baby-sitting and have left the entire field to the public educators. It is not our purpose to set forth the pros and cons of preschool and kindergarten training. There is an abundance of very substantial literature on the subject. But it is a practical fact that once a child is enrolled in a public kindergarten it takes a strong parent to transfer him to a first grade in another school. The pattern of enrollment suffers, and very often children of the parish are deprived of the benefits of Christian education because of the initial commitment to a public school.

How many children per classroom? A glib answer is, "The fewer, the better," but this ideal is seldom possible to achieve. For a kindergarten, 25 should be the absolute top figure, and an enrollment of 20 for single classes in the first and eighth grades. Double classes should not exceed 40 children. Many localities are governed by health laws which limit the number of children proportionately to the square foot area or the cubic volume of the classroom. It should be remembered that classrooms with too many students require an in-

ordinate amount of discipline, with resulting tensions among the children and the faculty.

What should be the cost of tuition? This is not even remotely an architectural question. Its answer belongs to the financial officers of the church. However, it is affected by the cost of construction, the amount of the mortgage, and the carrying charges. The architect may contribute some information in these areas, but the final answer must rest with the congregation. In this connection it is worth noting that there is one school of thought which believes that there should be no tuition fees, that the entire school operation should be subsidized by the parish church.

Where can reliable working information be obtained? Answers to this question are limited only by the amount of time available. The architect can do himself and his clients a great service if he can persuade them to accompany him to other district schools in operation, whether or not designed by his office.

The purpose of such a visit is not only to observe brick and mortar, floor finishes, windows and the inanimate factors but also to explore the functions and philosophy of the completed plant. An hour-long chat with a friendly, intelligent pastor or principal can be a revealing, gratifying experience. The local sexton is not a qualified witness. An initial planning or functional mistake in a pioneering field is understandable, but to repeat it endlessly is monstrous. Exchange of ideas will help avoid such occurrences.

Can anything be learned from public education? A great deal, and this opportunity should not be overlooked. Present indications point to a great revival of education under religious sponsorship. Whether public and religious education will work cooperatively toward a common objective is largely in the hands of the religious groups. Should they be inclined to offer the hand of good fellowship, there is no doubt that it will be accepted.

In plant planning, construction, and maintenance alone, the public groups have a wealth of hard-earned experience which they are willing to share.

What are the fundamental planning elements of a grade-school building? Of course, this is a question almost impossible to answer as a generality. But let us apply it to the six-classroom building discussed previously, which will have certain invariable elements basic to a minimal but complete school. It is to be understood that as the number of classrooms increases amenities and even luxuries will creep in. But for our six-classroom building we consider the following minimal:

One kindergarten with separate toilet room and separate small outdoor play area

Five classrooms — if only one story and on one grade, each classroom should open directly outdoors. This is particularly true in milder climates

Facilities for preschool and day nursery for working mothers (these will vary with location)

Toilets for boys

Toilets for girls

Health room, with adjoining toilet if possible

Principal's office

Office for school secretary

Small waiting room for visiting parents and registration

Teachers' rest room with small refrigerator and range

Toilets for teachers — separate facilities for each sex

Library — generous

Storage space — do not skimp this area

Wardrobes for pupils — in corridors or classrooms

Corridors — 8' 0" clear width

Entrance lobby — large enough to permit parents shelter in bad weather. Removal of rubbers, galoshes, etc., for smaller children takes time and space

All-purpose room — for chapel, recreation, lunch program, assembly, gymnasium

When an educational building adjoins the main church complex, it may be possible to use rooms on a multiple basis. Wherever possible, however, classrooms should remain inviolate with the exception of joint use with the Sunday school program. Evening use of classrooms for choir practice, teen-age programs, and the like has not proven successful.

2. Programming

As soon as the research and survey stages are complete, a definitive program of requirements can be established. Very often these two stages can be developed concurrently.

The program actually represents the specification for the full scope of the educational plant. It should develop immediate and future objectives, philosophical aims, physical requirements, and pupil and faculty availability. The last may not appear to be important architecturally, but indirectly it is applicable. There is no point in erecting a 12-classroom school if teachers are in short supply and if pupils can only be provided as they rise through the grades. This is an important factor, which should be carefully studied.

When the program is fully developed it should be set down in report form in careful, precise language and submitted to the congregational governing body for its approval.

3. Master Planning

Even at this late stage we are unready for final planning. The elements of the complete program should be set down in diagrammatic form. If the school is to be located completely apart from the parish church by which it is sponsored, then the planning problem is simplified but the cost will increase because of the duplication of utilities and services and the probable difficulty of school and church using certain rooms on a joint basis.

Wherever feasible, it is preferable to have church and school buildings located on the same plot without intervening streets. Circulation between the school and the chapel facilities should be fairly direct, and in colder climates such communication space should be sheltered.

The master plan should show schematically but definitively all existing construction, proposed immediate construction, and planning for the future.

Open site areas should be developed to indicate parking locations, recreational areas, areas for lawns and shrubbery, walks, and entrance doors to buildings. Street utilities should be indicated, and entry points of services should be designated. Street and lot line setbacks as required by local zoning should be delineated.

The master plan should not be the result of a casual effort. It will keynote the lifelong function and interrelationships of the building complex. It is as important to congregational life as the circulatory system is to a human being.

4. Preliminary Planning

The architect is now in full charge. Initial survey work and programming performed jointly with the building committee, pastor, and principal are now completed. The master plan is down on paper. Financial commitments have been consummated by the church. The architect has been instructed to proceed with the preliminary planning documents for the immediate project.

Preliminary planning is essentially a detailed extension of the master plan for that portion which is programmed for immediate development.

Under the previous stages the size of the school, the number of classrooms, classroom density, and similar factors have been established. The architect now prepares and submits to his client for review a preliminary design. This design is carefully evaluated by the client and, if found to be satisfactory, is approved. If the design is not satisfactory in every particular, the architect will revise it or, if necessary, develop a new design to the satisfaction of his client. The client should keep in mind that the sketches presented by the architect are, in the architect's opinion, the very best of many possible solutions he has explored. To consider and review more than one design at a time will only lead to confusion and subsequent delay in the project.

No detailed discussion concerning the preparation of final documents will be considered in connection with educational buildings, as the requirements for this phase are more or less standard for buildings of all types. References to this phase elsewhere in this volume in connection with churches will apply also to school facilities.

5. Site Considerations

The criteria and standards set forth herein for the acquisition of a church site are applicable to the educational facility as well.

Where local transportation is available, circulation to and from buses or taxis should preferably be localized adjacent to a main entrance to the school.

Parish responsibility and liability extend up to and often beyond the entrance to transportation. Hence the importance of continuous supervision of children until they are returned to the care of their parents. Lightly traveled streets are preferable for unloading and loading of buses.

Whenever possible, parking facilities for Christian day school and Sunday school should be separated from the normal church parking. Sunday morning parking lot confusion is not always conducive to a worshipful attitude. Hence the desirability of individualizing these facilities, particularly where evacuation and entrance to a parking area coincide.

Indoor and outdoor recreational space is essential to the completely equipped school. It is seldom possible to achieve this ideal in the form of completely autonomous facilities. There is no objection to dual use of the parking lot provided that there is no traffic during school hours, also provided that the paving is of a soft material less likely to inflict bruises and skin injuries when children fall. Permanent pavement markings and portable equipment will permit maximum use of such an area.

Safe intercommunication between church structure and school is essential. Where these facilities are separated by a public street it should be a secondary, lightly traveled thoroughfare, preferably with a safety light at the nearest public crossing.

Real Estate and Legal Guidance

The location of qualified sites and the exploration of legal ramifications lie in the field of trained experts. The services of a local realtor can be invaluable. Legal counsel is necessary.

Real estate law has roots which extend back into English history. Let no congregation feel that it can dispense with legal advice. Actually in many states a contract for land is considered invalid if not prepared by an attorney.

The road to land ownership is strewn with pitfalls in the form of defective titles, prohibitive restrictions, confiscatory easements and covenants, clouded ownerships, and other situations. The disclosure of such matters is second nature to the experienced attorney.

6. General Considerations

Some religious schools have begun to recognize the potentialities of audiovisual education. It is quite possible that the shortage of competent and dedicated teaching personnel will lead to a more general acceptance of this effective teaching medium.

Pending further development in this field, the school that is farsighted enough to equip itself with a separate, well-ventilated audiovisual room, empty conduit systems, and a control room for equipment places itself in the comfortable position of being prepared. This is a new field, unexploited in its possibilities, and bound to develop.

Classroom lighting has developed over the years into a science which must be applied judiciously to the areas involved. The architect and his consultants should be equipped to advise competently. But it should be remembered that eyestrain and fatigue can stem from too much as well as too little light. Where debate occurs between advocates of incan-descent and fluorescent lighting, the recommendation of the architect should be followed.

The desirability of acoustical correction should be determined by engineering tests, as all rooms for public use are improved by a certain amount of brilliance through reverberation as well as by absorption provided by acoustical material.

Where spaces are of unusual shape, great size, and varying densities, an acoustical treatment is an asset. Sound qualities can be regulated by proper disposition of resounding surfaces applied by engineering determination.

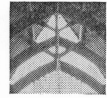

Chapter 10

RECREATIONAL AND PARISH FACILITIES

The propriety of the use of church property for recreation and other services normally provided by the community has long been a bone of contention within the various religious groups. During the latter half of the 19th century and well into the 20th various pietistic groups and congregations have remained aloof from the thought of intermingling social activities with the worship objectives of dedicated sacred property.

A great deal of the dissension derived from philosophies and attitudes developed in Europe and brought over to America by energetic mission-minded souls. Today we are faced with the fact that national population growth is reflected in corresponding church growth made up largely of native stock. The solid throng of European nationals of past generations has been replaced by a heterogeneous assembly of people stemming from totally unlike national and ethnic backgrounds. They all answer to the name "Christian."

The new parishioner, unfettered by old prejudices, feels free to look to his church for a full community and social life in addition to spiritual sustenance for his family. In democratic congregational church government it follows that the people are given what they are willing to work for, provided that it does not encroach on fundamental doctrinal tenets.

Hence the seemingly endless train of church construction carrying with it supplementary service buildings: recreational halls, multipurpose rooms, educational facilities, gymnasia, and the like.

The church today, as with the 13th-century European cathedral, becomes the central focus of the immediate community of souls. All eyes are focused in that direction — first for worship, and after that for education, and then for sociability and recreation. If people gravitate to the church for decency in their diversions, no man should turn them away.

The recreational facilities, when they are provided, should be planned to avoid encroachment upon worship. Economy may dictate that a single large area be designated for multiple use by the congregation. An auditorium-gymnasium is a sound concept, whereas a church-gymnasium is obviously unthinkable.

The large open room as a supplement to the church building is an invaluable asset. If possible it should provide clear open space devoid of free-standing posts or columns. The enormous popularity of basketball dictates a ceiling height of about 20 feet with floor dimensions permitting at least a public-school-size court.

A room of this size and height lends itself to layouts for badminton, volleyball, and hand tennis. One side wall of the room should be kept free of columns, low windows, and radiators to permit impromptu handball. The floor should be scored for these activities; also for shuffleboard and the traditional games for children from kindergarten age upward.

Toilet and shower for both sexes should be directly accessible from the gymnasium. These need not be elaborate and preferably should be kept separate from similar facilities normally in use by the congregation.

Basketball has an enthusiastic spectator appeal

particularly where interchurch competition can be arranged. Where funds permit, space for spectators should be provided. This requires a substantial area increase, which may push the cost of the structure beyond the purchasing power of any but the larger congregations.

A permanent stage or platform at one end of the area and a balcony at the opposite end can be used for spectators where area along the sidelines is not feasible.

An auditorium-gymnasium such as we have been discussing can be of inestimable benefit to a congregation and if properly planned and programmed can serve all age groups and both sexes. In addition to the uses previously discussed it can serve as an assembly room for Sunday school and Christian day school; meeting hall for religious gatherings and Bible school, dramatic presentations, church dinners and bazaars. But to make such space available on a rental basis for public use is a violation of the tax exemption privileges extended by the community to the church. As a good citizen the church must bear such considerations as these in mind and set an example rather than seek an undue privilege.

The large, open auditorium-gymnasium has limitations in its multi-use objectives. It is not well suited to small groups, or to subdivision into small cubicles for Sunday school or released time purposes. Its large proportions throw it completely out of scale for the simple requirements of preschool and kindergarten children. Subdivision of a high-ceilinged area is awkward, costly, and inconvenient. It is seldom satisfactory from the standpoint of classroom privacy.

Where the auditorium-gymnasium represents the second stage of construction, the first being the church, serious and prayerful consideration should be given whether a valid educational wing should not precede it.

The full impact of the church's responsibility in the educational field is beginning to be felt by American Protestantism. Where a denomination or an individual congregation is inclined to assume this obligation, there the educational plant should take precedence over the large multipurpose room.

Where no question of choice occurs, the auditorium-gymnasium should be built of the best and most durable materials. If funds are available, the floor should be of selected maple or birch installed to meet the latest specifications of local public

agencies. The floor-laying pattern must conform to the sports to be played. In rare cases where roller skating is permitted the floor joining must be designed accordingly.

If economy dictates the use of resilient floor materials, it is preferable to specify from the vinyl family although the pure vinyls are quite expensive. All resilient floors are put to an acid test from the impression of portable chairs and women's spike heels. Before making a choice of flooring it is advisable to check its actual performance under similar circumstances. Laboratory tests are generally inconclusive.

Walls of the all-purpose room are preferably of smooth surface masonry materials. Where body contact games are played, walls should be devoid of projections and rough surfaces. Heating units should be of the low baseboard type or else kept above body height. If the exterior architecture permits, windows should be at the top of the wall and protected by hinged interior gratings.

Ceilings with exposed structural elements are preferable to plaster or acoustical tile. Structural framing members are decorative in their simplicity and lend themselves to orderly arrangement.

Artificial lighting should be either concealed or designed to withstand the impact of a basketball. The lighting should be controlled to permit selection of a light level compatible with the activity of the moment. Dimmers are not the complete answer to the selective light level. A carefully thought out switching system may be just as effective and less expensive.

The promiscuous use of applied ceiling insulation materials is not justified except as a corrective measure after the space has been tried out for a cycle of uses.

The area and expense normally allotted to a stage platform and dressing rooms is difficult to justify when one considers the limited use of these facilities. But the alternative of assembling and disassembling this structure several times a year is much less attractive. The permanently erected stage is perhaps more palatable if it can be easily screened off and used as meeting space or a classroom. High windows along the sides can prevent the stage space from becoming a dark pocket. Stage lighting can be provided for effective performance at no great cost if purchased as part of the original installation. Wiring for public address and sound picture systems should also be considered. These will be more fully discussed elsewhere.

The portable stage has come into favor for religious drama performed either in its conventional location or in the round. This permits use of area otherwise preempted by the permanent stage.

No church building complex is complete without some provision for kitchen service. This may vary from a modest affair comparable to a domestic kitchen, to an elaborate and costly installation which would do justice to a modern restaurant. There is no rule of thumb which can be used to appraise local feeding requirements. In an average congregation the church dinner program calls for about five or six dinners each year. Where this entails food service for two or three hundred people, even the most modest meal puts heavy pressure on the kitchen. Church kitchens like public highways cannot be designed to meet peak load requirements within the normal economy.

The local situation should be carefully studied and the space and equipment requirements decided upon early in the planning phase. Even if the purchase of kitchen equipment is deferred, the mechanical requirements should be anticipated and designed into the basic building. Steam tables, automatic dishwashers, and large cooking ranges all affect the design of the kitchen.

Each kitchen, small or elaborate, involves fundamental planning requirements. Food and utensil storage, food preparation and food service, followed by dishwashing and garbage disposal round out a cycle which is normal to any mealtime.

Where the requirement is modest, the arrangement of fixtures may be left to the architect in collaboration with the building committee and a representative of the women's organizations. This may be a painfully tedious experience, but it generally produces a kitchen layout locally acceptable.

However, when elaborate facilities are required, with perhaps combined cafeteria service for a parish school, then the employment of an experienced kitchen consultant is highly desirable. A large, well-equipped kitchen represents a substantial investment. When it stands idle most of the time it also represents waste. But where a large investment is justified, there the cost of professional planning is in order. Active kitchens require a study of time and motion, circulation and cross circulation, preparation of food, disposal problems, and cleaning up.

The limits of parish activity are usually determined by the amount and suitability of space available. In addition to the large auditorium-gymnasium, there are other requirements which must be accommodated. A centrally located office is essential, particularly for any congregation interested in an active parish program. The office should function as a central point readily accessible to a street entrance and the pastor's study. Within the office, but preferably separate and adjacent, should be a room fitted out for publicity equipment, mimeograph machines and reproduction apparatus. Materials for the publicity operation should be stored within easy reach.

Even in the quietest parish the provision of at least two meeting rooms is essential for the normal functioning of church societies. These areas can be used on a multiple basis and are well worth the investment.

More elaborate facilities may be provided for parishes endowed with land area and funds. The council or voting body merits a board room, which can double as a counting room for the financial department, a school board room, a committee room, and at other times as a meeting room for pastoral conferences.

A generously sized room for teen-agers, fitted out as a club room and provided with facilities for music and hobbies and a "snack bar," can develop great popularity among young people and their parents.

Most churches lag far behind in providing for the social needs of elderly people. A sewing room for older women and a reading room for men would offer a form of therapy greatly needed today.

A quiet room for prayer and meditation, not necessarily a chapel, would offer to people of all ages a sanctuary away from daily excitement where just for a few moments one could be alone with God.

The outreach of the church today is limited only by the facilities it offers. Recreation and secular activity fall well within the scope of Christian life provided that they are disciplined in that direction. Physical and mental fitness are as important in the church community as they are in secular life.

Often overlooked in the development of additional physical facilities is the rather obvious fact that greater building volume automatically brings about higher operating costs. Additional space throws upon a congregation the responsibility of consistent adult supervision. To permit the use of parish facilities without proper programming and supervision is to invite deterioration of the physical plant and a corresponding breakdown in congregational life.

LIBRARY

One facility, not often included in the building program, is the Parish Library.

The Parish Library is becoming an increasingly important facility in every parish. Although the parish library is basically a resource library, it can contain fiction, poetry, humor, and other writings having a religious connotation. Under no circumstances should the library try to compete with the public library. If the parishioners are expected to use the library, it should be located in the mainstream of traffic — near the Narthex. Control presents a problem. The facility should be so located and arranged that all patrons are required to pass by the Librarian. A simple system of identification and checkout, similar to that used by the public libraries, should be instituted and maintained. The library in a small parish might consist of only a few shelves located near or in the Narthex. In the larger parish, the library could very well be a large room furnished with bookshelves, study tables, and some comfortable reading chairs. Such a room could serve several functions such as Bible study, pastor's classroom, meeting room, and so forth.

Chapter 11

CHURCH FINANCING

The end of World War II was followed by an era of church building unequaled in history. Modern technology combined with money readily available has permitted the development within a single generation of complete parish-church communities which in other eras would have taken centuries to fulfill. Whereas the 13th-century man was indeed fortunate if several bays of the village church were completed during his lifetime, modern man, more impatient, is satisfied with nothing less than full completion of the building in much less time.

Thus the modern era, notwithstanding its strains and tensions, has managed to recognize the importance of God in the contemporary scene.

The intense dynamism of contemporary life has directed a stream of energy and money into church construction. This energy, which is always present but sometimes dormant, has been revitalized and activated through God's will. Certain other ages in church history have been thus blessed. The ready availability of money, although flowing from the same source, presents a phenomenon to which modern man is unaccustomed. Religious groups at various times during their history have enjoyed periods of great wealth, but the concept of money as it has developed under the aegis of capitalism has been regarded by them with some uneasiness. R. H. Tawney in his fine study *Religion and the Rise of Capitalism* makes the point that the church in the 16th century was unable to reconcile itself to the idea of interest and under certain circumstances declared it sinful.

Variations of this attitude have carried well into the 20th century. Even through the present day certain denominations and individual parishes consider a mortgage as being a transaction outside of the ethical limits for religious bodies.

Banks and fiduciaries for decades regarded the church as a credit possibility first with suspicion and then with an air of patronizing sentimentality. More recently financial officials with their hardheaded practicability have come to understand that established religious groups exert a stabilizing influence first on the neighborhood, then on the community at large, and finally on the nation. While this attitude has little concern with bringing souls to Christ, it has nevertheless opened up the American credit system to the extent that the church can now fulfill its missionary objectives on the American continent.

Churches, parochial schools, and other parish facilities have flourished throughout the land by reason of the many-sided resourcefulness of enlightened capitalism.

A great abundance of support has come from the people through direct contributions, tithing, and memorial gifts. Many conscientious Christians take seriously the income tax deductions permitted by the government for contributions, and both they and the Kingdom are enriched thereby. But the individual parishioner is more than just a source of cash. He represents the ultimate basis for the extension of credit to the religious corporation. No matter how humble he may be, it is his honesty, reliability, integrity, and sense of Christian responsibility which is the financial core of the church, either by direct contribution or as an instrument of credit.

Direct contribution for building, which was in other years a rather simple matter of adding an extra section to the weekly envelope, has become much more complex and correspondingly more productive.

Just as modern public relations has become an extension of neighborliness, so the phenomenon of fund raising has been an outgrowth of what was originally designated as giving. Fund raising, in its most elementary and most dignified form, exists where the parishioner contributes in answer to a direct appeal from the pulpit or from the officers of the congregation without the inevitable pressure which attends a campaign. The direct appeal method, notwithstanding its obvious virtues, lacks the sustained effect required for a long-range program.

If the financial objectives call for a formal campaign, there are many who feel that it should be organized and staffed exclusively from within the congregational ranks. This method is patterned after the approach of the professional fund raiser without the payment of a fee to an outsider or exposure of the congregation to strange faces. This method has proven successful in many instances. It has also produced some notable failures.

The next most acceptable method lies in the use of experienced fund raisers, not affiliated with the immediate congregation but employed through the local office of the denomination. Normally a fee is paid for this service, but the fact that the money finds its way into the denominational treasury makes it more palatable to the local parish. There is much to be said for this method. Denominational sponsorship erases from the parishioner's mind any cynicism concerning the sincerity or pecuniary motive of the fund raiser in charge of the operation.

The final step in this discussion leads us to the professional fund raiser, generally a business corporation, national or regional in scope, well staffed and equipped with all of the most modern and persuasive techniques. Since the end of World War II professional fund raisers have done an enormous job for churches of all denominations.

Where their program is carried out with Christian dignity and without undue publicity or embarrassment to individuals, there is no more effective method for raising money. Because of his wide experience the professional fund raiser is able to approach the problem without lost motion and free of personal or preconceived sentiment.

Most fund raisers will work with a congregation without charge up to and including the point of evaluating its fund raising ability. This calculation is based on statistical experience and is arrived at by a study of the total communicant membership, annual budget experience, the economic level of the area, and other pertinent factors.

It is surprising that on the basis of simple statistical mathematics plus experience the potential figure is often far above the expectations of the local congregation and, more important, is so often realized when totals are consummated in the form of initial pledges and ultimate collections.

Fees to the fund raiser are usually a lump sum based on a fixed percentage of the estimated amount to be pledged. It is at this point that congregational storm signals are in evidence. In a large fund-raising campaign the fee could be substantial, and certain frugal parishioners will demur, quite understandably. Voices will be raised — "We can do it just as well or better by ourselves"; or, "The three, five, or ten thousand dollars we are paying *them* could equip our chancel"; or worst of all, "If they employ *them* I won't pledge a red cent."

It would be presumptuous if within these pages a foolproof positive solution were offered. Patience is a God-given virtue, and this is one occasion when one should pray that the supply runs deep and pure. So often the most vociferous objectors become the most vocal supporters. The power of prayer is unlimited.

Once a contract has been signed, the fund raiser should be given a free hand, totally unhampered, provided that the campaign is conducted in a manner not offensive to the religious community.

In the majority of instances the actual canvassing will be performed by members of the congregation under the direction of a professional. Occasionally the entire campaign will be conducted by individuals from outside the congregation.

There will be rallies, pep talks by the coach, kick-off dinners, victory dinners, prayers of thanksgiving, and occasional discouragements. It can be a period of wonderful Christian excitement with permanent effects on the congregation in improved stewardship and closer personal relationships.

The contract with the fund raiser should stipulate that he return to the congregation to revitalize the program if it bogs down. This obligation will be fulfilled provided that the congregation has followed instructions laid down by the fund raiser, who will maintain a constant personal relationship only during the pledging period, after which the contact tapers off.

Legal advice is never a luxury before a contract is signed. The agreement relating to fund raising is no exception. All of the questions should be asked and answered beforehand, and the fine print and the area between the lines should be thoroughly explored. Even honest misunderstandings tend to destroy business relationships. In fund raising all efforts must be directed toward the common goal and no energies needlessly expended in controversy.

Once the pledges are in hand the congregation is in a position to appraise its program in terms of overall budget.

Pledge payments cover a two- or three-year period, and unless some construction activity takes place during that period, collection of pledge money tends to slow down.

To cover whatever interim deficits may occur during construction or in the financial structure thereafter, it may be necessary to arrange for a permanent mortgage effective either during or after construction. The characteristics of the mortgage will vary in each situation. Certain denominations are rigidly opposed to the concept of God's property being subordinated to an agreement which could end in foreclosure and eviction. Others will not permit dedication of a church building until all mortgage obligations are discharged.

There is no uniformity in state laws concerning mortgage procedure or the limitations under which religious corporations may operate. In specialized transactions of this kind the services of an attorney experienced in real estate and religious procedure should be obtained. This is no field for amateurs or for experimentation.

Allowing for regional restrictions and variations, mortgage money is available from banks, insurance companies, building and loan associations, religious bodies, and individuals. The maximum amount of the mortgage is generally limited by statute to a percentage of the total value of a property. Lending institutions are disinclined to permit religious corporations to borrow up to that limit. This is a good thing for lender and borrower alike. A mortgage is sound only to the extent that it is buttressed by solid equity. The 15- or 20-year life of the average mortgage covers at least one dip in the business cycle. It is during this period that the inexorable

burden of top-heavy carrying charges can destroy the financial equanimity of any congregation.

In early English history mortgage was ominously defined as a death pledge, and as such it developed serious breaches between mortgagor and mortgagee. In the modern credit concept a mortgage, conservatively developed, can be a live, dynamic document.

Where the total sum of the fund-raising effort does not equal the amount of the total development cost, then the difference must be made up by: (1) contributions, (2) secondary fund raising, (3) sale of bonds, (4) permanent mortgage.

Permanent mortgage financing, where permitted by state law and denominational rubric, is the method most generally used in providing for additional funds. Generally, permanent financing does not take effect unless secured by completed construction.

This financial gap can be bridged by temporary funds derived from direct loans or temporary mortgages. It is understandable practice in financial circles to discourage temporary financing unless backed up by a permanent mortgage commitment, from which source the interim loan is satisfied.

The amount required for a temporary or permanent loan will vary with each situation. Prudent management will avoid top-heavy outside financing, as the carrying charge can be burdensome.

Temporary financing has one great advantage: It permits the initiation of construction work before all contributions and fund-raising payments have been completed.

In the ideal situation the building development should approach completion at the end of the building fund collection period. This implies that sufficient funds are available at all times to meet payments to contractors and for other costs normal to a construction operation.

In certain areas the construction of buildings cannot be started until all mortgage or trust deed papers have been signed and recorded in the county where the work occurs, and all moneys placed in escrow by that time in the full amount of the construction cost.

No contractor should be expected to wait for payment of his periodic requisitions without a complete understanding of such obligation at the outset of construction. A constant turnover in cash is indigenous to the building industry for payment for materials and salary. In rare instances a contractor may offer to finance a religious institution over a rocky financial period. By and large it is preferable to have the contractor current on payments. This leaves the architect with a free hand to enforce contract requirements. Creditors are not amenable to directives.

Temporary or interim financing provides the answer for those congregations anxious to proceed with construction with prudent diligence and careful haste. By this means, funds are available for regular payments as soon as the local coffers are depleted. The draw down upon temporay financing should be deferred until the last stages, as interest payments start with initial payment of principal. All financial institutions should receive certification by the architect before the releasing stage or before periodic payments during construction.

At the completion of construction and after the contractor has satisfied all contractual obligations including lien releases, the permanent financing takes effect, with its annual carrying charges becoming a periodic obligation of the congregational budget.

The financial community has extended the hand of confidence and cooperation to the religious fellowship, with the result of extending various financial techniques to religious growth.

Bond houses have explored the responsibility of religious groups and have been pleased with what they have observed. As a result, bonds backed by the integrity and reputation of groups of congregations are being offered in the financial highways and byways to a receptive market.

Finance is attended by as many pitfalls as building construction. It is no primrose path for the unititiated. Here again the payment of a fee for sound advice represents money well spent.

Just as physical planning requires the services of architect and engineer, so does financial planning dictate the employment of sound financial advice on the part of attorney, bond counsel, real estate or stock broker. The entire financial campaign should be as thoroughly planned at the outset as a Grand Tour through Europe.

Money changers of integrity are not out of place in the temple.

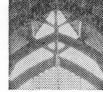

Chapter 12

PHYSICAL ENVIRONMENT CONTROL

We deal here briefly in a non-technical manner with various methods of controlling man's physical environment. By physical environment we mean those elements which affect his sense of touch, smell, sight, and hearing.

We know that Jesus frequently sought out ideal spots when He taught large groups. The temple and the synagog provided, to a limited degree, a controlled environment. There was privacy, visual and auditory, there was shade and a certain amount of warmth. When He taught out-of-doors it was usually in some secluded spot where privacy, comfort, and beauty were afforded His hearers.

With the development of mechanical means of controlling environment, man has become accustomed to and demands that surroundings be adapted to his comfort. He expects this in his house of worship and his schools. And this is as it should be, for worship and learning become more effective experiences in an atmosphere where distracting sounds and movements are excluded, where the air is fresh and of the proper temperature, where the spoken word and music can be clearly heard, and where clear sight is available without any strain upon the faculties.

Atmosphere more conducive to worship and learning has added to the cost of church and school, but it has proved to be a good investment. There is nothing unchristian about reasonable comfort, provided that it is not confused with indolence and self-indulgence. Let us not forget that modern technology is based directly on God's laws.

If the Christian is more dynamic and productive at 70 degrees Fahrenheit, then by all means let there be the mechanical equipment to achieve this result summer and winter.

Heating, Cooling, and Ventilating

Fuels

There are a variety of fuels used to heat buildings today — wood, coal, coke, natural gas, manufactured gas, oil, and liquefied petroleum gases. The day when we can heat with atomic energy may not be far off. Fuels are mentioned here only because the architect must know what fuels are commonly used in a community — it makes a difference in the type of equipment used. Sometimes more than one fuel is available, in which case cost and availability will determine which to use.

Heating Systems

Basically there are three types of heating systems: (1) convection, (2) radiation, and (3) a combination of convection and radiation.

Heating by Convection — Central System

Convected heat from a central system employs the principle of heating air and moving it to various parts of a building by means of ducts. This system has been used for many years in the heating of houses and other buildings of simple design. Heating a large building by this means poses many problems such as excessively large ducts, large fans, additional space required to contain these items, as well as difficulty in zoning for comfort.

In small churches and schools this system is fairly satisfactory. If ducts and fan unit are properly sized and ample space is allowed, summer cooling can be added without major change to the distributing ducts.

Heating by Convection — Unit System

The basic difference between the unit system and the central system is in the equipment used and where it is located.

In the unit system each space is provided with its own convectors, unit heaters, or unit ventilators. Heat is supplied to these units by means of a central steam or hot water boiler. The convector depends on the natural movement of warm and cold air to heat a space. From this it is obvious that convectors are not entirely satisfactory for heating large spaces. Both the unit heater and the unit ventilator are equipped with fans which move the air. The unit ventilator has the added feature of being able to bring in the proper amount of fresh air.

The unit system makes it possible to have individual room control of the heating. Summer cooling can be accomplished with the unit system if it is properly designed.

The convection system (forced warm air) has the added advantage of being able to provide tempered or cooled fresh air for ventilation during seasonal changes.

Heating by Radiation

Radiant heat is the oldest method employed by man to heat his shelter. It goes back to the campfire of the tribes of Israel. The Romans employed it to heat their public baths. Modern man is trying to tap the original source of radiant heat, the sun, to heat his buildings.

Radiant heating systems most used today are those which, by means of hot water coils buried in the floor or electrical resistance coils incorporated into the floor, walls, or ceilings, warm the surfaces of a room. These warmed surfaces in turn radiate heat to objects and people in the room. This type of heat develops very comfortable warmth. If it is the only source of heat in a building, it is not totally satisfactory because it does not provide the necessary ventilation. Mud tracked in on floors heated by radiant heat soon becomes dry, and a dust problem is created. Radiant heat has been most successfully

used in swimming pool areas and outdoor stadium heating. The recently developed quartz heat lamp offers new possibilities in heating exposed areas such as porches, entrances, and outdoor spaces. Radiant heat is especially helpful in "spot" heating of certain areas of a building, particularly those remotely located from the central heating plant.

The Combination System

Architects and engineers have long been aware of the shortcomings of a purely convection or radiant heating system. Early attempts to design a combination system left much to be desired due to a lack of proper equipment. Today the designer has excellent equipment and controls with which to work.

The modern combination system can supply air at the desired temperature to any space in the building. The system can heat one space and cool another simultaneously. It can provide the proper amount of fresh air. It will exhaust offensive odors. Humidity can be controlled at a comfortable level. Normal filters will keep the air relatively free of dust. Special filters can be provided which will eliminate pollen. Supplemental radiant heat will warm cold surfaces such as walls and windows. A properly designed and installed combination system will provide complete comfort zoning.

Comfort Zoning

It is rather obvious that rooms on the east side of a building are going to be warmer in the forenoon than rooms on the west side. In the afternoon the west rooms will be warmer than the east rooms. In the northern hemisphere rooms on the south will be warmer than rooms on the north. Interior rooms may require no heat at all. Rooms on intermediate floors of a building will require less heating than the top floor. Basement rooms will require little heat. Rooms containing a large number of people will require less heat, but more cooling, than those housing few people. Rooms having a large amount of glass will require more heat and cooling than those having little glass.

Providing a satisfactory year-round air-conditioning system which will produce uniform comfort for this complex set of conditions has led to the development of equipment and controls of a rather complex nature. Present-day equipment will cool one space in a building and heat another space both at the same time. This is what is called "comfort zoning."

It can be as complex or as simple as desired. However, it should be very carefully engineered by a competent professional mechanical engineer. As intimated previously, the system can be designed to include summer cooling, as well as heating. In those areas of the country requiring only cooling, the heating cycle can be omitted.

Another feature of such a system is that fresh air can be introduced into the system, in fact, up to 100% of the required amount. This feature keeps the air fresh and free of odors. On mild days the ventilating feature provides air at the proper temperature without use of heat or cooling.

Another point to be considered is the comfort of people sitting close to an outside wall. Such people will feel uncomfortably cool on a cold day. This can be overcome by installing a radiant heat element along the base of the wall. The cold draft that falls off windows can be tempered in a similar manner.

Equipment necessary to accomplish zone heating and cooling is made by several manufacturers and is not unreasonable in cost. Although this system can be made almost fully automatic, the custodian should be instructed in the operation so that a malfunction can be detected early and corrected before serious trouble develops.

Heat Pumps

In recent years the heat pump has made its appearance. Simply stated, the pump extracts heat from the air in winter for heating purposes. In summer the cycle is reversed for cooling. If the outside temperature drops above or below certain Fahrenheit limits, it is necessary to supplement the heat pump. This makes it more suitable for moderate climates. Heating and cooling systems employing the heat pump are classed as convection-type systems. Supplemental heating is usually accomplished by means of electrical radiant heat. The heat pump should be given consideration where electrical power is very cheap or other fuels are difficult to obtain.

Other Considerations

Adequate insulation of both the building and the heating system is important. Such insulation is relatively inexpensive and will pay for itself in fuel saved.

Quietness of operation is a highly desirable feature of a heating system. Water hammer in pipes, the hissing of air at a vent, the roar of a fan, or the cracking and popping of ducts is very distracting and unnecessary. Quietness can and should be built into a system.

When determining the design criteria for the heating, cooling, and ventilating ssytem, it should be borne in mind that the installation will be as permanent as the building, and that it is difficult to replace it. Equipment that has a shorter life than the building should be placed in the building in such a way that it can be removed and replaced easily.

A good hot water or steam system will outlast a furnace system but will cost more.

If a summer cooling system is to be added to the heating system at a later date, the system must be designed to accommodate it and space must be allowed in the building for the additional equipment. The architect should be reimbursed for the design of the cooling system even though it is not to be installed for some time.

A conscientious architect will secure the services of a competent mechanical engineer for the design of the heating, ventilating, and cooling system.

Lighting and Electrical Systems

In the realm of lighting of buildings we are just beginning to emerge from the "dark ages." In our churches we still see light fixtures that were originally designed to burn candles or oil, modified to contain an incandescent lamp. We continue to think of lighting as something to be applied after the building has been designed. It should be designed as an integral part of the building. We should be concerned as much about the quality of light as we are about the quantity.

Lighting Classrooms

It has been said, and illuminating engineers still agree, that the perfect light for a learning task is under the shade of a tree on a bright sunny day. Here you have light containing the full spectrum, you have it in ample quantity, it is free from glare, and it is well diffused. There aren't enough trees to go around, and not all days are sunny; so the next best thing is to simulate this condition indoors. Considerable progress has been made toward this goal. It is not difficult to recall the days of the classroom lighted with one or perhaps six incandescent lamps.

Today the generally accepted standard for classroom lighting is 35 footcandles. Light under the "tree" will measure about 1,000 footcandles. Today it is practicable to have 50 to 70 footcandles of light in a classroom. In the not-too-distant future, levels up to 100 footcandles will be feasible.

In some learning tasks, color perception is important. Therefore a light source that duplicates natural sunlight is desirable. Today the deluxe cool white fluorescent lamp is the closest approximation of natural light.

Tasks that involve three-dimensional objects are best accomplished when harsh or multiple shadows are eliminated. This is best accomplished by well-diffused light, producing single, soft shadows. A light source that produces glare also produces eyestrain and body fatigue, thereby making more difficult the learning task.

Of the four qualities of good lighting mentioned above, quantity is the least important; however, the ideal is an ample quantity of light from a source containing the full spectrum, free from glare and well diffused.

The fluorescent lamp is the best and most economical light source on the market today. However, it must be installed properly or it is little better than a bare incandescent lamp. The tube should be shielded so that it cannot be seen. This can be done with a lens or louvers. In general, a direct-indirect fixture suspended 12 to 18 inches below the ceiling will produce a fairly well-diffused light. Surface-mounted fixtures that emit light along the sides as well as the bottom do a fairly good job. Fully recessed and bare-tube fixtures require special handling to reduce contrast and glare.

One of the finest developments in lighting in recent years has been the "luminous ceiling." It is costly, but eventually the price will be more reasonable. Such a light source is produced by installing bare-tube fluorescent fixtures 12 to 18 inches below the ceiling. Below these fixtures is then installed a diffusing ceiling of glass, plastic, or louvers. If properly designed and installed, the "luminous ceiling" is an excellent light source.

Special consideration should be given chalkboards and walls. A shielded two-tube fluorescent fixture, mounted above and extending the full length of a chalkboard, does an excellent job of illuminating the work surface. Walls illuminated in the same manner can do much to increase the light level of the room, as well as make the room seem larger.

The best lighting system in the world is of no value if the surfaces of the room are ignored. Desk tops should be of a light color so that contrast between the desk surface and the work is minimized. Desk tops should have a dull finish so that the image of the fixture is not reflected by the top. Ceiling colors should be light in color to reflect the greatest possible amount of light. Walls and floors should be of colors that have a high reflectance factor. Highly reflective surfaces such as gloss enamel, stainless steel, mirrors, etc., should be avoided. Dark or primary colors, introduced for accent, should be limited to not more than 10% of the wall area.

Controlling natural daylight in the classroom is a difficult thing to do. Many different things have been tried — directional glass block, shades, blinds, roof overhang, sun screens, special glass — but none really solves the problem. A number of windowless or nearly windowless schools have been built. This may solve the problem, since it is relatively easy to control artificial light and ventilation. Total elimination of windows may not be desirable and is not recommended; however, window area can be greatly reduced to advantage.

Lighting the Church

Very little data has been compiled and no standards have been established for the lighting of a church. Any discussion on this subject will consist principally of an expression of opinions and not of facts. Perhaps it is well that no standards have been established, because standards tend to stymie growth and development, and church lighting has not reached a point of development where it can afford to be stereotyped. There are, however, certain basic principles which should be observed in this field.

Lighting, if properly used, can change the apparent size and shape of a space; it can establish and change the feeling of the interior envelope; it can create moods; it can direct attention; and it can be used symbolically. In preparing the program of needs for a new church project, lighting should be given as much consideration as music or other amenities of worship.

Consider first the purely functional relationship of lighting to worship. It is important that people be able to see well to enter and leave a building. Concern for the well-being of every worshiper dictates that stairs, ramps, and exits be well lighted. Reading, at certain times by certain people in certain places, is a part of every worship service.

A good lighting system will provide a sufficient amount of light in these places at the right time.

The color of the light becomes important when it is realized that color can make a congregation or minister appear healthy or quite ill. An excessive amount of blue light, whether it comes from fluorescent lights or from blue glass in the windows, does not flatter the complexion.

A concern for the comfort of all worshipers will prevent the placing of bright or glare-producing light sources (fixtures or windows) in the direct line of vision of any participant.

It is important at times that attention be directed to different parts of the church, i. e., the cross, altar, pulpit, lectern, font. Light can be used effectively to accomplish this.

Light can contribute to any desired mood. A feeling of joy can be created by its abundance. The feeling of solitude or mystery can be created by a low level of light. The drama and mystery of worship can be greatly emphasized by creative lighting.

Just as proper lighting can enhance a worship service, it is also true that it can detract when improperly designed. It is therefore important that lighting be given adequate study commensurate with its important place in worship.

The lighting needs of different denominations will vary. An order of worship which involves a great deal of drama will require a lighting system more complex than a service which contains little or no drama. An example of extremes might be a Roman Catholic service compared with a Friends service. The Anglican and the Lutheran order of worship contain a great deal of drama. As other denominations tend toward more formalized worship, the need for compatible lighting effects becomes more urgent.

Stage lighting techniques and equipment can be used to accomplish desired effects. Such techniques should be used with skill and moderation in order to avoid artificial effects, often offensive to conservative parishioners.

Lighting equipment available today provides the designer with unlimited possibilities. As architects and congregations become aware of the relationship of light to worship, there will be much experimentation — with both good and bad results. The results will be improved if both the architect and congregation try to develop a better understanding of light in its relationship to local liturgy and worship.

Natural Light in the Church

Since there is a trend today to use large amounts of glass and since most worship services are held during daylight hours, a few words on natural light in the church may be appropriate.

Natural light is excellent because it contains the full spectrum of color. This spectrum is modified when the light passes through colored glass. How it is changed depends on the designer. Natural light emanates from one source, and that source travels a fixed course. It is more difficult to control natural light; however, it can be controlled by the location of openings, roof projections, sun screens, and various mechanical devices.

In the 4th century, after official recognition and acceptance of Christianity, Emperor Constantine ruled that churches should face east, the chancel west, in order that on certain days the entrance portals could be thrown open for the rising sun to cast its first shaft of light through the length of the church to terminate on the altar. This was a direct extension of pagan ritual; it came to an end when the orientation of cathedrals was completely reversed. But it did recognize the awesome majesty of the solar cycle, which today we incline to ignore as though it did not exist. This is no plea for a return to solar worship. Rather it is an appeal for a recognition of the place of the sun in daylight and a further appeal that churches be oriented to accept the full beauty and glory of sunlight.

Whether natural light, artificial light, or a combination of both is used in church illumination, an intelligent study of the lighting needs should be made and, where funds permit, a competent illuminating engineer should be retained to assist the architect in securing the desired results.

Electrical Distribution

Many fires in churches are caused by faulty or inadequate wiring. Most of these troublesome installations were made many years ago before safe standards were developed. Congregations are unconsciously creating hazards today which will result in tragedies a few years hence. In a desire to minimize construction costs the electrical system is frequently cut to a minimum. In a short time after the building is finished the deletions are forgotten and additional electrical equipment and appliances are added to the system without regard to its capacity. It is not uncommon to see extension cords run exposed to provide additional outlets for unanticipated equipment. Overloading of circuits causes overheating of the conductors, which results in a deterioration of the insulation. The next step is the "short" which causes the fire.

Where future special electrical requirements can be anticipated, provision should be made for an empty conduit system built into the original structure.

Public address systems, electronic organs, moving picture apparatus, and telephone installations all require electrical wiring. These facilities are often installed by specialists after general construction work is completed. A simple empty conduit system extended to a critical point will permit the avoidance of exposed wiring and cutting and patching of finished installations.

The total cost of the electrical system is such a small part of the overall cost of a building that it does not pay to skimp on this part of the structure. The service entrance, service entrance equipment, distribution equipment, feeders and panels should be oversized in order to handle loads that may be added in the future. Every electrical system should be designed by a competent, licensed electrical engineer. Circuiting and sizing of equipment and conductors should not be left up to the electrician, nor should an electrical system design be prepared by a contractor or electrical supply house. The architect should secure the services of an electrical engineer, thoroughly experienced in his field.

Acoustics

In a church or classroom it is important that the spoken word and music be heard clearly. It is also important that distracting noises from adjacent rooms and from the outside be eliminated.

The acoustical qualities of a room depend on its size, shape, and surface treatments. Sound isolation depends on the materials of the structure.

Acoustics in Churches

The large cathedrals of Europe were beautiful structures and were acoustically excellent for the monumental organs built into them; but they were not satisfactory for preaching. Preaching was not an important part of worship in those days; hence there was no great problem. The Word of God has become an important part of the act of worship for almost all denominations today and must therefore be given prime consideration.

It is generally acknowledged that the acoustics of a church will be reasonably good, for both voice and music, if the nave is about twice as long as it is wide and if the materials of the walls and ceiling are neither too hard nor too soft. It is not always feasible or desirable to build in these proportions.

The development of new materials and construction techniques makes it possible to construct a church in any one of several shapes and sizes. These new forms have introduced problems of acoustics which cannot be solved by "rule of thumb" methods. However, the science of acoustics is sufficiently advanced that there is no longer an excuse for poor acoustics in any church. If a church design is unusual in form, the services of an acoustics engineer should be secured early in the planning stages.

A church that has excellent acoustic qualities for voice may very likely have poor acoustics so far as the organ is concerned. Generally an organ sounds better in a building having hard reflecting surfaces, and this is less desirable from a speaking standpoint. Where doubtful acoustical situations arise, it is preferable to lean to an interior that is too brilliant acoustically, as it is easier to control a lively room than to step up a cushioned area.

In many instances the quality of the organ can be improved by making the opening to the organ chamber large enough, by proper location of the organ, by exposing the entire organ, and by putting in an organ of the proper size.

There is at least one organ installation where the pipes are located in a basement room quite remote from the congregation. The music is picked up by several microphones and "piped" through an amplifier to a cluster of speakers in the nave. Naturally the quality of the music will be no better than the amplification equipment. Although this method of developing compatibility between music and the spoken word has not been perfected, it is worthy of consideration and experimentation.

Quite often poor acoustics for music is blamed on the building, when in reality the organ may be too small and of a poor quality.

An excessive amount of soft material such as carpeting, acoustic tile, and drapery can have an adverse effect on the acoustics of a building. Many congregations, in an attempt to correct bad appearance, have created a worse condition by covering the entire ceiling with acoustic tile, thereby deadening it.

A factor frequently ignored is the sound-absorbing qualities of the clothing worn by the worshipers. An empty church may seem too "lively" but, when filled with people, it may have excellent acoustics.

It is possible to vary the sound-absorbing or sound-reflecting qualities of building surfaces by means of mechanically operated louvers or shutters, one side of which may be covered with a soft material and the other side with a hard material. Resonance chambers which can be opened and closed at will would also be an asset.

Acoustics in Classrooms

Acoustics in a classroom present an entirely different problem. Teachers are often young women and have soft voices. Various activities take place in a classroom simultaneously. Classrooms have almost doubled in size in the past decade. Classroom ceilings were once quite high (10 to 12 feet). Now they are frequently no more than 8 feet high.

Too much acoustical treatment can make a classroom so "dead" that it is depressing and very difficult to teach in. By the same token, a room that has nothing but hard reflective surfaces tends to sustain sounds, which creates an equally unsatisfactory teaching situation.

It has been found that porous, lightweight masonry blocks have desirable qualities for classroom wall construction. Acoustic tile and plaster ceilings, if not overdone, can be beneficial in maintaining a low noise level.

If hard finishes are used on walls, then it is advisable to use a highly absorbent material on the ceilings. Draperies on windows can also serve to dampen noise.

Sound Transmission

As stated earlier, effective worship and learning is somewhat dependent on the elimination of external distracting sounds. These noises may come from the adjoining room, the playground, the street, or nearby industry.

There is a common misconception that materials that will absorb sound will also reduce sound transmission. The control of sound transmission is a matter of mass and density.

Thick masonry or concrete walls are most effective in reducing sound transmission. Lightweight, hollow masonry blocks are not always effective barriers to sound. Normal conversation will travel right through these walls unless they contain special aggregates.

Lath and plaster partitions are fairly good at retarding the transmission of sound. Special sound-retarding partition and ceiling systems, utilizing spring clips, have been developed and are fairly effective.

It is important to remember that if a mechanically suspended acoustic tile ceiling is installed, the partitions between rooms must be built solidly to the floor construction above. If this is not done, noise will travel from one space to another by going through the ceilings and over the intervening partition.

Another unsuspected conductor of sound from one space to another is the ductwork of a heating system. To overcome this, all ducts should be insulated on the inside. Runouts from the main duct should have two or three 90-degree turns. Sound traps can be built into ducts, but these are expensive.

Some early handbooks on construction recommended a partition constructed of offset double studs with a blanket of insulation woven in between the studs. Recent experience has proven this construction to be relatively ineffective as a sound stop.

If a church is located where there is an excessive amount of neighborhood noise, it should be planned and designed to minimize sound infiltration. Solid masonry walls, having few windows, will help eliminate distracting noises. Light frame construction should be avoided if possible. As mentioned previously, concrete is an excellent retardant material for most sound frequencies. Snug-fitting solid-core doors are much more effective at stopping sound than hollow-core doors. Double glass is far more effective than single glass.

During the initial site planning, orientation of the building should be considered as a means of minimizing the infiltration of outside noises.

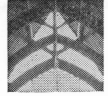

Chapter 13

CHURCH PROPERTY MANAGEMENT

To those who have lived through the creative and building stages of any portion of church building operation the dedication service may symbolize the completion of a job well done in the name of the Lord.

And certainly the members of the building committee and congregation who have conscientiously and prayerfully guided the project, whether church, school, or recreational facility, through the irritations and uncertainties of construction are entitled to their sigh of relief and the gratitude of the congregation.

But it soon becomes apparent that, instead of being completed, the job has just begun. Even buildings erected of the most desirable materials begin to deteriorate the day of their initial occupancy. Care, adjustment of mechanical equipment, and cleaning must start immediately.

Granting that the physical church in all of its many aspects is erected to the glory of the Lord as a house of God, it is also true that it must offer to the worshipers all of the comfort, shelter, and amenity found in any other type of abode.

Pagan worship was conducted with the people out-of-doors and the priestly caste domiciled within the shelter of the temple or sanctuary.

Christianity from its earliest beginnings in the synagogs of Jerusalem and shortly thereafter within the protective underground confines of the catacombs consistently has held its worship indoors, away from the disturbing influences of the outer world.

The Biblical invitation, "Let us go *into* the house of the Lord" has been joyfully accepted and in its fulfillment has produced great works of art not only in cathedrals but in humble wayside churches and chapels.

Indoor worship carries with it the obligation to provide adequate and continuous protection against the elements — a perpetual and seemingly one-sided struggle of man against Nature. In most cases "man" assumes the shape of sexton or janitor — very often an overworked, self-effacing saint, but perhaps just as often a hair shirt to congregation and pastor.

Where this is a trouble area in parish life the fault does not necessarily lie with the individual. More likely it stems from a lack of recognition of the overall problem.

The enormous increase in the number of new churches combined with the technical complexity of even the smaller church plant has placed the problem outside of the scope of any single employee. Management is as urgently needed today in the operation of the religious plant as it is in commerce.

Good management calls for intelligent and experienced administration. And while many clergymen are generously endowed with administrative talent, it is an established fact that no seminary or divinity school on the North American continent offers a degree in stationary engineering. This is as it should be. To expect or even permit a pastor to tinker with thermostats and other modern installations is to foster a waste of time and talent.

The management responsibility of the church property properly must be assumed by the congregation. It is a complicated matter involving the employment of personnel; the continuous supervision of plant and employees; the keeping of accounts;

legal and insurance matters; public relations among maintenance staff, pastor, and congregation; public relations with community and neighborhood; and the keeping of records.

This could very well be the agenda for a real estate organization, which in effect it is. The Bible makes numerous references to keeping one's house in order, and the house of God is certainly no exception. Unfortunately, it is a directive largely misunderstood or ignored by the average parishioner. As a result its fulfillment is often the hit-and-miss product of well-intentioned but fumbling efforts.

Good real estate management for a church requires competent direction at the house committee level. A pastor blessed with administrative judgment will aim to have this committee consist of three or four men who individually or collectively are good public relations men, possess some technical knowledge, and have a sense of values. If one or two of the committeemen are gifted with mechanical ability combined with the will to keep busy about the church property, so much the better.

In a national economy which permits fairly early retirement very little has been done to provide the avocations required to give the retired person a sense of responsibility and accomplishment. Many such persons, men particularly, wither on the vine.

The congregation should be scanned for people who have time on their hands, are blessed with the urge to produce, and — most important of all — offer a Christian attitude in their dealings with associates and subordinates. Work on the church property can be dramatized validly as an effort in the vineyard of the Lord. Many will respond to this approach and gain stature and spiritual comfort thereby.

However, there are limits to what the volunteer can be asked to do. Put a man on a lofty extension ladder with a paint brush in his hand and he will be happy, productive, even though uneasy. This is adventure! Place the same man on the floor with a broom or mop in his grasp and he becomes a janitor.

The constant, menial jobs required to keep the church household sweet and clean must be performed by a regularly employed individual, and where the plant is of great size by a staff.

This leads us directly into the subject of the sexton.

The sexton can trace his lineage directly to the early church. Then known as the sacristan, a position of great dignity, he took complete charge of the sacristy with all of its sacred appointments. Just as his title was corrupted over the years, so have his functions deteriorated, in the eyes of many, to a janitorial level.

Today a stigma is attached to a job which was once a position offering stature to the man who held it. The result of this unfortunate situation has been the virtual elimination of the long-tenured dedicated employee, respected by all, and his replacement by a kaleidoscopic succession of inept individuals totally unable to face the disciplines of a tough job.

In his fine, sensitive study of a Catholic priest, *The Edge of Sadness,* the author, Edwin O'Connor, introduces his readers to one Roy, the sexton of Old St. Paul's Church. Were Father Kennedy not already overwhelmed with the acute problems of parish life, our friend Roy could be considered a masterpiece of comic relief — a hair shirt answering to the name of Falstaff. But he is much too close to his living counterparts to be a joke.

The fact that we permit the Roys to hold down jobs for which they are not equipped reduces the position to an absurdity and drags down the pride and stature of the thousands of men and women who have served the Lord so well.

In a smaller sense the sexton should fulfill the specifications previously set forth for the house committee. Above all he should be a person of unlimited industry and infinite tact. But the congregation should be quick to recognize that even the most dedicated individuals can be overworked. If a single sexton is obliged to operate and maintain a complete religious complex — church, school, and recreation building — it is quite apparent that he will not remain with the congregation for long, and if he does remain he will be old long before his time.

Merit must be recognized in terms of salary, housing, and complete acceptance into the religious and social life of the congregation. Anything less than that is not enough.

When the proper relationship exists, house committee and sexton operate as a team, the first calling the signals and the second doing the heavy ball carrying. When the work load is overwhelming the house committee should be alert to the situation and provide the necessary relief: volunteers for snow removal, lawn mowing, and holiday decorations; mechanics for heavy plumbing and electrical repairs; professionals for cleaning stained-glass windows, refinishing architectural woodwork, and caring for expensive landscaping.

The sexton, if conscientious, will have enough to do if the normal chores are fulfilled. Cleaning, arranging for services and parish activities, supervision of the grounds, cleaning again, minor repairs followed by more cleaning — this is the story of the sexton's life. If he is a well-organized individual who can adjust his routine to the seasonal requirements, then the house committee is free to devote its efforts to church year programming and long-range maintenance work where outside contracts are involved.

A sexton may be highly industrious but in need of direction. In such a case supervision falls to the lot of a member of the house committee who conveys to the sexton the wishes of pastor and congregation. Patience can be a deeply rewarding virtue where language or intelligence barriers impede communication with the sexton.

A simple written schedule of the general routine of the church coupled with a description of the sexton's related responsibilities will be enlightening to all and will minimize duplication of supervisory orders which countermand each other. Where the line of authority is properly drawn, the sexton is chargeable to the house committee and not to the pastor.

Selection and purchase of maintenance materials should be by the sexton, but quantities should be audited and inventoried by the house committee.

Where existing installations such as wood or resilient floors, cabinet work, and installed artwork require special care, manufacturers' instructions should be followed. When the scope of a job lies outside of the abilities of the sexton, paid professionals should be called in. It will be much less expensive in the long run.

Every church plant should be fitted out with a small but well-equipped workshop. Tools and equipment should be of good quality, kept under lock and key, and inventoried periodically. Likewise there should be adequate storage — dry and well ventilated — for holiday fittings, draperies, and general appurtenances. No frustration equals the futile, last-minute search for the knickknacks of yesteryear. These too should be kept locked up and clearly labeled for convenient future use.

All transactions within the jurisdiction of the house committee should be recorded and made available to the congregation.

Deeds, surveys, architectural as-built drawings, and other documents relating to the church property should be stored in a fireproof vault along with the church charter, constitution, and the basic historic papers of the original parish.

Where legal matters are encountered, no matter how minute, they should be referred to an attorney. Proximity to God does not relieve the church of its normal obligations to the community. In a court of law a religious body can expect no preference. Land acquisitions, contracts, agreements, important transactions, loans and mortgages have traditions going back to English common law. This is no area for the amateur. The legal profession is prepared to serve any religious denomination competently and without extravagant charge.

As the church enlarges its plant and property it is faced with many more of the problems found in secular situations. Closely akin to business in its dealings, the church must follow the better business practices.

Insurance is a prudent business protection which the church must include in its portfolio. Here again the amateur should be subordinated. Insurance is far-reaching in its benefits, but without guidance the premiums can be costly. A general insurance man within the congregation or an outside consultant should be engaged to prepare a total insurance program. This should include fire and extended coverage, theft, liability, window breakage, automobile, and any other applicable property insurance. Where a parish school is operated, teachers and students should be insured properly to reasonable limits.

Wherever possible, the entire church staff — pastor, teachers, organist and sexton — should be included in a comprehensive insurance plan covering accident, sickness, and death. Where denominational pension plans are available, these should be extended to the entire personnel. Social benefits today are available throughout all areas of business and industry. The minimal wage which is generally paid to religious workers dictates that a reasonable security program be maintained in their behalf. While this may not seem to be related to operation of the physical church plant, it is an important manifestation of goodwill from the congregation to the church staff at all levels.

Goodwill is presently known in the world at large as public relations. It is represented in all areas of life by well-trained men and women who present their vocations to the public in the best possible light. In its worst form it can be cynical and insincere; in its better manifestations it has brought about a more sympathetic understanding among groups widely diversified in their views. Religious groups have developed their public relations conscientiously and to good effect.

The local parish church should have some sense of public responsibility toward its neighbors and the community. Externally the plant and grounds should be kept in top condition: buildings freshly painted, lawns and hedges trimmed, landscaping controlled. In the wintertime sidewalks should be kept free of snow and ice; throughout the rest of the year walks should be kept free of leaves and debris.

Exterior public address systems and carillons should be used at worship hours only, and then perhaps muted. Parishioners should be urged not to congregate for long periods on the public walks surrounding the church property; Sunday school children should be forbidden to run and shout throughout the church neighborhood.

Where a congregation is blessed with wide frontages on one or more streets, a public gesture particularly appreciated can be made by planting trees along the curb. Virtually all communities will assist in the selection of trees conditioned to local atmosphere and climate and further will maintain them after they are planted.

An alert house committee can be of indispensable assistance to a building committee and architect when new facilities are in the planning process. A complete record of experience gained from previous construction activities should be displayed for the benefit of forthcoming operations. While subsurface investigation has become an accepted requirement in advance of construction, it is not always reliable on a year-round basis as an indication of groundwater levels. Experience with past wall and floor leakages, settlement cracks, and foundation defects, if properly diagnosed, may forestall a recurrence of the problem in new extensions to the existing plant.

Local vandalism and damage caused by mischiev-

ous children may help determine the location of exterior walls; heavy winter frost may dictate the design of footings for exterior steps and walks; plaster may be susceptible to damage in certain locations within the building; the high cost of painting may justify an investment in aluminum for exterior windows and door frames.

A free exchange of ideas between house committee and building committee can result in substantial operating economies for the future.

This chapter has touched lightly on the many-sided aspects of church management. It is readily apparent that an entire volume could be devoted to it. The Roman Catholic Church, by reason of its centralized authority, has done outstanding work in this field by assembling operating data based on actual experience and conveying this information to parish priests and architects during the planning of new developments. In addition, mass purchasing of maintenance materials and equipment has resulted in real economies.

Other denominations, in which congregational life is more autonomous, have less opportunity to observe trends in the field of operation, and their buying power is much smaller. To offset this obvious shortcoming local ingenuity must be invoked. Technical and management people within the congregation should be brought into the house committee; several neighboring congregations may join in mass purchasing; motor-driven lawn and snow removal equipment may be shared by neighboring parishes even when of differing denominations.

Several top-grade church management publications are published periodically. There are several Roman Catholic publications exclusively devoted to the subject, which are available by subscription. By observation, study, and exchange of ideas a house committee member can develop management know-how closely approaching the professional level. It follows that such training is not expendable. Housekeeping in God's house may well become a lifetime avocation, enriching the lives of those who serve in order that others may worship in comfort and cleanliness.

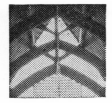

Chapter 14

MUSIC AND THE CHURCH PLAN

"Then was our mouth filled with laughter and our tongues with singing." (Ps. 126:2)

"Speaking to yourselves in psalms and hymns and spiritual songs, singing and making melody in your heart to the Lord." (Eph. 5:19)

Old and New Testament alike make music an essential part of religious life.

Music in the church should be regarded not as an extraneous artistic interruption but rather as a ministerial function in the service of God.

There cannot be good music in the church without people dedicated to its production and, equally important, facilities for adequate and dignified preparation and performance.

The training of a disciplined and artistic choir, at once a part of and yet subordinate to the worship service, is not without its frustrations and tribulations. More than one clergyman has referred to it as the "War Department."

But the present vista across the American musical landscape is one full of hope and encouragement. The entire North American continent is overwhelmed by the sound of music.

Radio, television, high fidelity and stereophonic sound deliver a continuous message in music. Admittedly a great deal is of dubious quality, but the human ear is being exposed to music as never before.

Music, some of it dreadful, is being used to promote commodities. Music, much of it of highest quality, forms the background for mediocre films at the theater and on TV. No meal is complete in a better restaurant without a background of well-chosen music. Popular music — frantic, excitable,

and often of lowest possible taste — nevertheless does offer to young new composers a wide area for experimentation and exercise.

Paralleling apparent round-the-clock activity in secular music is a powerful renaissance of interest in the music of the church — traditional and modern.

Seminaries and conservatories emphasize the importance and beauty of religious music. Attention of the trained young clergy is focused more and more on the place of music in the worship service; graduates from the music schools are turning to choir direction, organ playing, and the composition of religious music; a host of parishioners are recognizing the cultural and religious value of choral participation in worship.

America may be entering its greatest musical era. The completely planned church must offer suitable facilities to make its contributions to one of the greatest and most popular of the arts.

The liturgy, the hymns, the anthems contribute to the unity of the service. To be effective they must be rendered in an atmosphere which is worshipful and at the same time compatible with the organ and the human voice. A lively acoustical interior is essential for Christian worship.

The basic shapes and the relationship of chancel and nave should be responsive to the audible elements of the service. Unusual geometric shapes often create acoustical problems, as do improperly curved surfaces. While the public address system has been a boon to the clergy, it cannot be readily adapted to choral singing, nor does it lend itself to the pipe organ.

For congregational singing the nave must be illuminated properly, either by natural or artificial light or a combination of both. Nothing can discourage congregational response more rapidly than light improperly disposed. Hymnals should be in large-size type, with music and words preferably presented in combination.

Music literacy is high among those who fill the pews. The hymnal is one area in church music which tends to remain static. The hard-cover, bound volume is so often a compendium of musical archaeology which closes the door irrevocably to further effort in a field so fruitful from the Reformation through the 19th century. Has the last great hymn already been written?

The choir, which has traditions antedating Christianity, deserves far better treatment from the building committee and architect than it often receives.

Currently it is receiving recognition in the form of growing debate concerning its location. The deep traditionalists claim that the historic antiphonal background places the choir and organ in the gallery. Those influenced by Anglican practice in this country insist it be in the chancel. Either location can be rationalized. Therefore it is not the purpose of the writer to take a strong position in favor of one or the other.

Where there is antiphonal exercise between minister and choir there is justification for a gallery choir with the congregation located between the two.

The unseen choir carries with it the mental suggestion of an angelic chorus, a mood not difficult to convey if the worship service is dignified and mystic and the soprano section is on pitch. Here again a crisp, clear acoustical setting is all-important.

The gallery reduces the choir to individual anonymity, it lessens the impulse for soloists to showboat, it removes from the congregation the antics of the histrionically disposed music director.

Where a choir is not sufficiently disciplined (and this is unfortunate in any location), the slouching, squirming, whispering, and giggling is perhaps less offensive in the gallery than elsewhere.

A tardy choir member can tiptoe into the gallery choir ranks unnoticed, provided that floor and furniture construction is sound enough to prevent telegraphing squeaks to the congregation below.

Perhaps the single greatest disadvantage of the gallery lies in its lack of adaptability to the short processional and recessional, the most graceful and dignified way to escort the clergy to and from the chancel.

In this respect the chancel choir is unequaled. There is no situation in Protestant worship which offers a better opportunity to unify the service than the processional hymn accompanied by a trained, well-groomed choir leading the pastor into the chancel. The processional hymn combines pastor, congregational, and choir in the initial stage of worship. When properly executed it sets a solid foundation for the remainder of the service.

When the processional choir reaches its place in the forepart of the chancel, the planning should be sufficiently ample to permit the individual choir member to reach his pew without interruption and confusion. Choir pews should be widely spaced (3' 4" between pews and at least 2' 0" allowed to seat each person). Rising and sitting cannot be accomplished gracefully if robed people are sitting haunch to haunch.

Pews must be generously fitted to hold hymnals, liturgical music, and anthems for normal services and a greater volume of music for recitals and holiday occasions.

Whether directed by organist or separate choir director, adequate visual rapport must be maintained for proper direction. Where choirs are massed, facing each other, then a simple system of mirrors should be installed for the benefit of the group not facing the director.

Organist and choir director preferably should be screened off from view by the major part of the congregation. Excessive arm waving or dramatic antics, by-products of accompaniment or direction, are of dubious value to the musical quality; they add nothing to the dignity of the worship service.

Previous references to the importance of clear acoustics apply with special emphasis to the chancel — it should have bell-like brilliance and clarity. Chancel draperies and tapestries may be pleasing to the eye, but they invariably render liturgical chanting and the prayers virtually inaudible. There remain certain portions of the service which are not well adapted to a public address system. Hard materials (wood and stone) are therefore preferable to soft materials for the chancel.

Lighting in the chancel should recognize that the Scriptures and prayers, the liturgy and music can be better delivered if they are legible. The lighting industry has produced splendid spotlighting inoffensive to the eye and yet functionally efficient.

No discussion of the robed choir can possibly be complete without an urgent plea for proper dressing and storage facilities. To the uninitiated, the choir procession with its starched robes and quiet demeanor represents the full fruition of the musical ministry — relaxed, dedicated Christians pouring out their hearts in song to the Lord.

Actually, choir work, not unlike the other arts, is full of tensions and also occasional flashes of temperament. The average volunteer choir has among its members family people of all ages, many with immediate responsibilities which inevitably accompany them to the choir dressing room just before worship starts.

Here bedlam often reigns, with members of both sexes in various stages of disarray prior to robing, a welter of clothing, swirling robes, hymnals, liturgical material, music for the day. Where there are multiple services, often one group is disrobing as a later group prepares for its presentation. This is not the ministry of music; this is confusion.

Where the choir has meaning to the congregational worship it is entitled to permanent accommodations answering to a reasonable standard of minimum decency. Each sex should have its own dressing areas and separate toilets, and there should be a rehearsal room for preservice exercises. Where local finances permit, separate accommodations for the youngest junior groups will lessen confusion between services and theoretically will permit some degree of preservice meditation by the senior choir groups.

A recent Associated Press story demonstrates the great dedication and certainly the extreme precariousness of life in a volunteer choir:

CHOIR ADDS VOICE DURING SERVICE

"Thomasville, N. C., Oct. 30 — A new voice was added to the choir at a church in the Midway community near here last night.

"During the evening worship service a baby was born in the choir loft to a member of the choir. Mother and child were taken to a hospital, and both were doing well."

This is perhaps the ultimate argument in favor of the gallery choir!

The choir director (or directress) is no longer the local piano teacher, worked into church service be-

cause of the illness or death of a similar predecessor. This statement is not intended as derogative of generations of dedicated but sometimes limited persons who by their perseverance kept American music from deserting the church.

The modern director is first of all a musician thoroughly grounded in the musical history of the immediate denomination. He is also a diplomat, public relations man, voice counselor, and an iron disciplinarian with a sympathy and love for his choir members. Above all he should have a definite opinion of the spatial requirements of the church to serve the best interests of the musical program, present and future. During the preparation of the building program he should therefore be given full opportunity to specify the requirements of his ministry.

After the architect has been engaged, the choir director should be consulted continually as the building program is translated into actual planning. He may be temperamental and demanding, but it is far better to discuss his requirements in open committee before rather than after the preliminary plans have been approved.

If we acknowledge the important place of music in Christian worship, then we should be willing to provide the facilities for its production.

Under ideal conditions the choir director should be supplied generously with an office, several rehearsal rooms, practice rooms for individual instruction, choir robing rooms (both sexes with toilet facilities), ample storage space for robes of all sizes for all choirs, and — most important — an adequate organ. It is difficult to dramatize the importance of a good organ when every building dollar has already been allocated to brick and mortar, but it constitutes a vital part of the structure.

The extent to which these facilities can be provided or planned for will vary with each congregation. But it is vital that all aspects of the musical department be discussed early during the programming period and the accepted requirements incorporated in the master and preliminary planning. Only in this way can music be given its due place in the church.

The current demands of the exploding population exact such urgent demands upon the budget for building volume that there is little left for important embellishment and amenities.

It would be difficult for the average parishioner to justify the omission of one or two classrooms in behalf of supplying the newly established church with the initial stage of a pipe organ. Hence many congregations initiate their musical objectives with small reed or electronic organs.

It has become somewhat fashionable for musicians and choirmasters to affect a snobbish aloofness toward electronic organs in general. Actually this type of organ, if properly designed, can render better service and deliver a greater variation in tonal quality than a small pipe organ. The electronic organ requires a knowledgeable organist, one familiar with the qualilties and also the limitations of the instrument.

One indisputable advantage characteristic of the electronic organ lies in its broad range of volume plus it flexibility in being piped to remote locations on the church campus. In addition, there is a strong possibility that continued research in the fields of sound and electronics may yet develop the compact electronic organ to a point where its sound production may rival that of the pipe organ.

There are many who would dispute such a possibility on the basic premise that the pipe organ is traditionally indigenous to the church. It is difficult to argue historical fact. Nevertheless where electronic organs are selected for reasons of economy of funds or space, the architect and building committee should study carefully the positioning of the tone cabinets in proper relationship to the size of the nave, size and location of the choir, importance of the liturgy, and the size of the organ. Electronic organs lose their tonal quality when too small for the area served.

Prudence would be served best if all churches were master-planned in anticipation of the future installation of a pipe organ.

Even the most modest pipe organ should have a generous allotment of space for pipes, chambers, console, and necessary mechanical equipment.

Organ builders are often unreasonable in their demands on the congregation for locations, areas, and sound-reflective wall, floor, and ceiling surfaces, very often to the detriment of other aspects of the church plan. Nevertheless to ignore reasonable recommendations of the organ builder will result in measurable loss of efficiency and tonal quality. It does not take a scientist to conclude that, if the sound output of a pipe organ is directed across the narrow width of the chancel perpendicular to the long axis of the nave, the sound which finally flows from the chancel into the nave must be somewhat in-

direct and distorted. To put it crudely, the $30,000 organ is delivering $20,000 worth of music in terms of purity of tonal quality.

Most organ builders will designate the gallery as their first choice for the location of pipes and supporting apparatus; second, the chancel altar wall directly facing the congregation. In either case the space requirements must be built into the building in advance if future alterations and makeshift compromises are to be avoided. Pipe organs, like church buildings, lend themselves to expansion; therefore the building should be planned to accommodate the long-range organ program. This will not involve extravagant allocation of building areas.

The location of the console, whether for pipe or electronic organ, involves planning ingenuity. Ideally the console should be in view of choir and clergy. In addition the congregation and the main narthex entrance should be visible to the organist. To accomplish this without exposing console and organist in full view of the congregation may dictate the use of screens and mirrors.

A shelf or cabinet for books and papers within arm's reach of the organ bench is an indispensable asset.

When the organ installation must be completed simultaneously with the church building, it is essential that the organ selection be made as early as possible. Organs, unlike any other musical instrument, may require complex attachments to the building and its services. Where such requirements can be included within the basic construction contract, much financial grief can be avoided.

In localities where organized labor exercises control, installations relating to the organ may be claimed by various trades. Jurisdictional disputes, walk-offs, and strikes could jeopardize completion of the entire building.

Wherever possible, the organ should be installed after the building has been completed and the various tradesmen have left the building. However, basic services and connections should be provided in readiness for attachment to the organ parts. Nothing can be more frustrating to clergy and congregation than the sight of completed work being cut into for unforeseen installations.

The fact that this chapter has dealt with the physical requirements of music in the church at a prosaic level does not lessen the fact that music is perhaps the greatest and most exalted of the church arts. Its artistic production relies as much on inspired planning and design as on great musical leadership.

All church art should be, in essence, anonymous and completely subordinate to the main focus of worship. Therefore the architectural setting for music should be quiet and unobtrusive. Fine cabinet work for organ and choir stalls, good lighting, and — above all — crystal-clear acoustics offer a suitable background for the ministry of music.

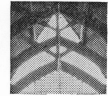

Chapter 15

COLOR

The blue of the sea and sky, the gold of the sunset, the entire color palette of the rainbow, and the glorious colors of God's creatures should arouse everyone to the truth of God's love of color.

Only man wallows about in drab, dull surroundings. Only man closes his eyes to the beauty of nature, and creates ugly places in which to exist.

The Gospel of the love of God toward men should bring cheerfulness, warmth, and happiness into the heart and soul of man. This should be reflected in his house of worship. This should be reflected in a harmonious symphony of color.

The violet, red, green, and white of the seasons of the church year are symbolic for the periods of time they represent. The appearance of these colors is enhanced by proper background colors. Thus they should be considered in the color design of a church. Color selection is an art and a science; it has psychological as well as physical effect on the beholder. The total color scheme should be carefully studied under all conditions of light and shadow, daylight and artificial lighting. Orientation of the building, size and shape of the areas, kind and color of the windows are all matters for consideration and careful study. Color effects and intensity will vary with latitude; with the direction and intensity of natural light; with the volume and quality of artificial light, whether fluorescent or incandescent.

Certain colors cannot be selected successfully until the building is nearly completed, including the installation of stained-glass windows, the lighting equipment, and various other items affecting either natural or artificial lighting.

Other colors which will have a direct effect on the final results must be selected earlier, usually in the design stages, as they form a part of the building process. These would include the marble for the altar, baptismal font, or other work; terrazzo or other integral floor materials; and exposed brick or stone surfaces. Furnishings and the various items connected therewith should be included in the total color scheme.

Certain manufactured materials — ceramic tile, linoleum, asphalt and vinyl floor tile, vinyl and other plastic wall coverings, and carpeting, for example — have certain fixed color and pattern characteristics. Rooms using this type of material should be studied in the light of these limitations when color schemes are determined. Colors should not be selected until the material to be used has been definitely specified.

Colors are selected on the basis of contrasting or complementary color combinations. A brilliant contrasting or an accented complementary color may be used to highlight areas requiring a definite "punch."

Colors of natural woods can be selected to bring out the best tones and grains of the particular species used. Natural wood tones augmented by highlights of definite contrasting colors can bring forth a vibrant, interesting surface.

In many instances colors which are decorators' fads are used because "this season it's gray" or whatever color is in vogue. This should be avoided at any cost. For churches and other buildings of a permanent character, color selection should be on a more concrete basis than the color fads of today, since new tones of color will be the style tomorrow.

The yearly restyling typical of the automobile industry illustrates this approach, which is aimed at making last year's model look strange and obsolete.

Be bold about color. There is nothing more satisfying than to be definite and forthright in color selection. Color can make or break a building design. It can indicate a weak indecisiveness or a bold definite conviction of being right. Right not only with the world but, more important, with God.

So use color boldly and reverently.

Chapter 16

MODERN METHODS AND MATERIALS

During the recorded centuries of building, places of worship were always constructed of the materials at hand or most economically available. These materials were assembled by the methods with which the builders were acquainted. It is obvious that the buildings of the past were built by plan. In addition to this, they were built under the direction of someone qualified in the art of building. The temple of Solomon could not have been built by a hit-or-miss method. The fragmentary evidence available today in Biblical passages and archaeological research indicates conclusively that a definite plan and method of construction was in effect. As an example, the stones were accurately cut at distant places; yet they fitted perfectly at the site where they were delivered.

After all these centuries building committees and congregations and even higher officials in various church organizations fail to examine carefully and plan for the use of the materials best suited to each individual project. Frequently no thought of permanence, maintenance, or real economy is evidenced.

In this century of progress there are those who would deny the Lord a proper dwelling place. In this day of fabulous new methods and materials, many are building the "slums" of tomorrow in church and Christian education buildings. Many are not considering the propriety of the materials used, nor have adapted them to local conditions. When lumber was in great abundance in our land, we wasted it. Today, through God's grace, technical men have found ways to put the available supply to better use. It took a world war to bring into being glued laminated wood beams and arches. Adhesives

had to be developed to bind together slender strips of lumber into beams, girders, and arches of sufficient size and strength to span large areas economically. As a result of much research and experimentation there are today available to the architect and engineer a variety of arches, beams, and girders of glued laminated wood at economical cost for use in the construction of beautiful houses of worship. A whole new concept of shape and form has been opened to the thinking designer. Other developments include 3″ and 4″ double-tongue-and-grooved sheathing capable of spanning larger roof areas without intermediate support. This is a breakthrough for simple, clean-cut interior ceilings of natural wood unhampered by intermediate purlins and rafters. Not only does this reduce material costs, but more particularly the cost of installation. All of this at no loss of safety or beauty.

Plywood has long been a standard product on the market, but new developments in adhesives have revolutionized uses for exterior as well as interior uses. Hardwoods of all types are available in plywood, providing beautiful finishes in natural wood for any purpose. Parabolic arches and folded plates of plywood have provided interesting spanning materials.

Possibly the greatest advance in materials has been evidenced in concrete. Again it required a world war to awaken the industry out of its complacency. This awakening also proved a boon to peacetime construction. Among the necessary types of equipment developed were large movable cranes and lifts capable of handling up to 65 tons or more of weight. This permitted the development of precast concrete slab design. Concrete panels can be cast at ground level and with these cranes or lifts put into position in walls or roofs like toy blocks.

In these precast panels all reinforcing steel, electrical conduits and outlets, or other structural elements can be installed at ground level. Supervision is simplified, and generally the total cost is greatly reduced due to very little use of form lumber and other items in the total construction of each unit. Surfaces of various materials such as ceramic tile, exposed aggregate, or other effects can be incorporated into the precast slab, providing a versatile finish for any surface.

Lightweight aggregates used in the concrete mix have made possible a more flexible use of concrete in a precast form. An idea as to the value of lightweight aggregates may be realized by comparing the normal weight of concrete at 150 pounds per cubic foot with lightweight aggregate concrete of the same strength weighing from 104 to 107 pounds per cubic foot.

A further development and indication of the flexibility of concrete is the thin-shell hyperbolic paraboloid arch. In Europe and South America the technique of the thin shell with the inverted curves has had a long head start on American attempts. However, there are many examples of this new technique in the United States. The hyperbolic paraboloid form may vary from a saddlelike roof to a total hyperbolic shape, or it may be of curves formed between triangles or quadrangles. The curved form may be an inverted umbrella or parabolic shape. In all cases the stresses act in a similar manner and permit a concrete thickness of from 2″ to 3″. The areas spanned by this type of construction vary from small distances to over 300 feet in clear span. This provides an open area within which any arrangement of space may be made.

Prestressed concrete is another recent development, and can be used in areas of similar sections with great economy. It involves the use of precast sections, with the reinforcing prestressed before the concrete makes the final set or hardening.

Each of these concrete systems should be investigated by the architect or engineer for its value for the particular project at hand. Precasting is difficult where there is insufficient space at the building site. Thin-shell structures should have proper location and backgrounds for their particular use. A thin-shell structure would lose its effectiveness in a built-up community; on a high hill with unobstructed view it is a wonderful addition to the community. Prestressed concrete should be used on projects of sufficient size to provide duplication of units. The overall economic picture should carry a great deal, if not the decisive weight in deciding what methods to adopt on each program.

To maintain their position in a competitive market, steel companies have developed new lightweight sections and connections. New and more complete test and inspection methods have made this change possible. The development of corrugated steel decking and other major advances have made this old standby material a competitive item in church construction. Welding has added further versatility to steel construction.

Structural aluminum with its lightweight advantage has made its appearance in construction. Windows, doors, jalousies, and railings have been available for many years and have proved their worth. Now structural design data is being developed for the use of aluminum sections.

In certain areas of the country reinforced masonry, brick, or concrete block have come to the fore. The cost of carefully designed buildings in these materials is generally less than that of other conventional types of buildings. Maintenance of these buildings is particularly low.

Closely following the development of thin-shell roofs, domes, and hyperbolic paraboloid arches came the necessity for lightweight, indestructible roof coatings. The plastics industry has come to the fore with plastic coatings for these steep, curved concrete surfaces. This leads to more new materials.

Plastics of various brands and names have appeared which bid well for the construction industry. The resins, polyvinyls, urethane, and other plastics add many new materials to the designer's palette. Structural plastics are being developed which should be available shortly.

Floor coverings, including asphalt tile, vinyl asbestos tile, vinyl, polymerite, and others, present colorful, good-wearing, and economical surfaces. Some are greaseproof and fire-resistant. Carpeting and fabrics woven of modern fibers are handsome, durable, and acceptable for use in certain areas of the church.

Paints have gone through a complete metamorphosis. Rubber-base, alkyd, vinyl, aluminum, and other plastic-base materials are providing surface coverings in competition with older materials. Low-fire-spread paints have been developed for areas requiring greater fire protection.

New methods and materials will continue to be developed. Each should be checked carefully for compatability with local climatic and structural conditions.

Fire- and stain-resistant countertop surfaces have long been available. To these are being added new tones, patterns, and wood replicas.

Acoustical treatment of churches has become a science. With various types of materials available, it requires an engineering analysis to determine where and how much material to use in a given circumstance. It should be remembered that good sound in a nave requires reflecting surfaces as well as absorptive materials. It is well to analyze the room for speaking voice, congregational singing, and organ music reverberation periods. Acoustical materials should not be indiscriminately applied on all surfaces. For large indoor places of assembly it is often desirable to defer installation of acoustical correction until after the space has been completed and its acoustical behavior observed.

Lighting is a science with many new facets. Dimmer controls for nave lights should be considered. Fluorescent lights are economical in operation and appropriate in classrooms and offices. Buildings should be studied for indirect lighting where possible. New fixtures are coming on the market daily, so selections should be carefully made. Electrical services should be ample for future electrical loads, as air conditioning, heating, ventilating, and organ blowers have to be included in electric power provision.

Heating and ventilating should also be the subject of careful study. Separate zones should be established for areas according to occupancy and use. In certain areas air conditioning should be used. Heat pumps are practical in many situations. This reversible cycle of alternately heating and cooling is available in electrical or gas-fueled units. Controls should be automatic and arranged so as to be foolproof. Installations having a complicated heating, ventilating, air-conditioning, and electrical system should be under the control of a mechanical maintenance man as well as a janitor to properly care for the system.

The most satisfactory sound system should be selected for the church. Low impedance with synchronized speakers properly distributed is favorable in some instances. Others prefer high fidelity systems emanating from two principal sources.

The installation of public address, sound, and intercommunicating systems deserves careful consideration. The public address system may be confined to the nave of the church, or be extended to serve other areas in the building. It may be combined with the sound system so that a common audio system serves to amplify the pastor's voice, recorded music on tape or discs, and the sound system of motion picture projectors.

The intercommunicating system is usually separate from the public address and sound systems. It too can be as limited or extensive as the size and nature of the building complex dictate.

It is of utmost importance that conduits properly located and of sufficient size be installed during construction of the building, even though they may not be used immediately. A ruby-red signal light at the organ console controlled from both the pastor's sacristy and possibly from the narthex (for use in weddings) is a necessary feature.

Another installation which can be an economy, particularly in planning areas, is the closed circuit television system. This is particularly desirable in the mothers' room, toddlers' room, or for overflow spaces. Such an installation permits the location of these rooms in areas other than adjacent to the nave. This frequently pays for the equipment and installation, because of economies effected by location at less expensive parts of the building.

Recently there has been a renaissance of stained-glass work. Stained glass set in concrete or plastic admixture has been brought to the fore. This is sometimes called faceted or chunk glass. The glass itself is from one to two inches thick, set in concrete. Designs of symbols, figures, or abstracts are made directly by the glass with no painting or firing required. The interior edges are chipped, thereby creating facets of light much as a gem is faceted. The windows have great depth of color and appeal.

Mechanization has reached the building industry. Mechanical equipment to do the handwork formerly required has developed with amazing rapidity — fork lifts and endless belt conveyors for handling materials, plaster installed by gun, lumber fastened to concrete or steel supports with cartridge guns, concrete jetted into foundations, electric tools for drilling and sawing, the trencher for digging foundations and trenches, and the bulldozer for moving earth or making cuts and fills.

These recent methods and materials have drastically affected the construction of buildings as well as their appearance. If used properly, and planned for from the start, new methods and materials will make better use of the stewardship dollars in church construction. God has enlarged the palette — may building committees, architects, and engineers be enlightened to have the imagination and good judgment to apply this blessing to His glory and to the advantage of the Kingdom.

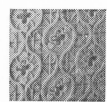

Chapter 17

THE INNER CITY CHURCH

As the population explosion continues and the automobile grows in use, the inner city has had great changes occur within its area. Some of the changes are fortunate in that they have cleared away slum or other undesirable areas, or caused the situation for traffic flow and parking to improve. Others have been less fortunate in the final consequences, and have caused unsolved problems.

One of these problems, with which many are greatly concerned, is the rapid decay of the inner city church. Churches which were the largest and best equipped have dropped in membership and evangelical drive to levels which cannot maintain the facilities or command the spiritual interest of new ethnic groups.

In some areas the encroachment of industry and subsequent population shifts have been the direct cause of retrogression. Other areas which in the prime years of a particular church consisted of beautiful residences have gradually gone down the familiar path of residential deterioration and final decline into slums.

Some well-endowed congregations still serve metropolitan areas of the large cities, but these are the exception rather than the rule. The reasons for the flight to the suburbs have been well publicized. They require no repetition.

What shall be done about the inner-city church? Structures which are substantially and well built can be remodeled and modernized to continue in the Lord's service. True, the future congregation may be of a different group of God's children, but the enthusiasm that can be engendered will maintain a virile inner-city fount of the Lord's work.

The church at large must realize that it should play a dynamic role in the inner-city area as well as in the newly developed suburban centers which are springing up each month. People of the inner city need spiritual nourishment. For these also are the church fathers of the future.

The challenge is great. In many instances the only impetus required is an intelligent and vigorous program of activities from worship to Christian education, from youth work to senior citizen projects.

City religious buildings erected during the latter part of the 19th and early 20th centuries benefited from the availability of fine masonry and carpentry materials at relatively low cost. Skilled mechanics and artisans, trained in Europe, were in abundance, and the combination resulted in buildings of great durability.

Only in the western hemisphere are religious buildings deprived of their longevity by reason of assumed obsolescence. Residual value is discounted in its entirety. This is a serious fallacy.

Every city and village in the United States and Canada is blessed with historic or semihistoric buildings, many of frame construction, which stand with great dignity and pride after a century of useful existence. It should not be forgotten that any well-founded structure, built with integrity and of honest material, is virtually indestructible. The great enemies of long life in buildings are fire and neglect, and the answer to these may be found in perpetual vigilance and intelligent care.

It does not automatically follow, however, that where an old building is considered for rejuvenation and modernization it will necessarily meet all contemporary demands. Nineteenth-century architects and builders entertained rather droll ideas about stairs, exits, and sanitary facilities, and did not fail to express them with enthusiasm.

Realistic soul-searching must be invoked where older religious buildings are to be continued in operation. Building code officials are notoriously generous in overlooking the most flagrant deviations from good practice where religious organizations are involved. This misdirected kindness places on the congregation and its advisers the responsibility of policing their own precincts.

Stairways and their enclosures should be of noncombustible materials, fire cutoffs provided to prevent the horizontal spread of fire, doors enlarged and created to facilitate rapid egress. Obsolescent heating plants and electrical systems should be replaced or renovated, draperies and carpeting flameproofed.

Where children are involved, the problem of fire protection becomes critical and, therefore, the criteria for safeguards should be most exacting. Within our time the most sobering recollection is that of the frightful human devastation of the Chicago parochial school fire. An entire nation wept with compassion for those who died and the parents who grieved. And yet, how few Sunday schools conduct fire drills and are conscious of the fact that the threat of destruction through fire is present just as much on Sunday morning as on any weekday.

Once the temperature of a fire reaches a certain flash point, it ignites volatile wall coverings and paints which generate gases toxic to the human system. This is one of the ever-present threats in the older building. Innumerable coats of paint offer a feeding area for the voracious appetite of fire out of control.

It does not follow that age disqualifies a building at any time, no more than advanced years infringe on the productivity of a human being. But we must recognize the inexorable toll of obsolescence and depreciation, and make reasonable Christian allowances. God has made laws which control human and physical behavior. These apply to all entities — animate as well as inanimate.

The old building may need a spiritual transfusion which extends its life into an era which differs completely from that of its original concept. And let no man say that the last state of the building is not better than the first.

The inner-city property falls within the compass of God's inventory. The product may be usable but somewhat unwieldy.

It is not intended within these pages to supply the ultimate answer. This calls for prayerful consideration, combined with a deep feeling of compassion and understanding for our fellow Christians.

The problem of inner-city rehabilitation is no longer the exclusive responsibility of religious bodies. Governmental and social agencies have awakened to the realization that unlimited outward expansion is unfeasible from the standpoint of communication, transportation, and services. The eyes which have been staring at the horizon, no longer unlimited, have been deflected to look backward toward the point of origin.

Redevelopment and urban renewal programs, however cumbersome, have begun to leave favorable imprint on the deteriorating core of our urban areas. The church must recognize the unique opportunity offered. Within these programs, there exists the possibility of increasing the area of the church site for recreation, parking, or building expansion. The house of God need not huddle in the midst of slum and blight.

The admonition to teach all nations applies as much to the foreign-born family on the other side of town as it does to an obscure village on the equator.

Here God has brought an extraordinary mission opportunity to a ready-made parish, complete with church plant and a mellowed Christian tradition. Many of these properties require only an open door and dedicated leadership.

The 19th century was the era of great social reform in the western hemisphere, and victory was won by individuals and groups against appallingly bad conditions. Today conditions not nearly as bad and much more receptive to improvement are challenging established parishes. We must be prepared to follow God's direction to equip our neighbors for acceptance of the responsibilities of the Christian community.

An equal responsibility rests with the religious leadership. Where the old parish is being revitalized, this process must be developed with competence and thoroughness. Halfway measures are not enough, particularly where the existing plant inventory lends itself to complete modernization.

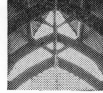

Chapter 18

THE BUILDING OPERATION

Religious organizations at the congregational level normally are not too well equipped by experience or personnel to cope with the uncertainties and frustrations of a construction operation.

Philosophically, however, they are, or should be, fortified with other strengthening qualities which should not be overlooked in the pragmatic business environment in which every construction operation exists. No congregation of any religious persuasion can overlook its basic responsibility to deal with justice and honesty in secular as well as spiritual matters.

Even the smallest building contract is attended by situations involving fundamental business relationships and basic principles of historic contract law. Accordingly it should be an accepted policy that all transactions are to be conducted on the highest plane of business practice, all agreements to be in writing, legal matters to be discussed with an attorney, real estate affairs with a real estate broker, insurance with an insurance broker. This will be further discussed.

Let us assume that plans and specifications have been completed by the architect and accepted by the building committee after a careful review concerning all aspects of the job. A statement of such acceptance should appear in the minutes of the building committee, and the architect should be formally notified of this fact.

At this point a quick review of essential conditions is in order, prior to the initiation of bidding procedures.

Have all building department, fire department, and other municipal approvals been obtained? Virtually all communities, rural and urban, require filing and approval of plans indicating their conformity with local building regulations. It is essential that such approvals be obtained prior to the award of a construction contract and preferably before bidding. When state codes overlap laws of villages, cities, townships, and other political subdivisions, it is important that the bidding documents comply with the more drastic applicable requirements. It is the architect's responsibility to advise the client of this connection.

Have all legal aspects of land ownership been satisfied? There have been numerous occasions where buildings have been erected on land not under complete ownership or where title is clouded. This is essentially a legal matter and, if properly transacted during the earliest stages of land acquisition, there should be no embarrassing loose ends. Nevertheless, a double check should be made to establish site boundaries definitely; to reaffirm clear title; to be assured of the absence of hidden codicils and easements restricting the use of all or a portion of the land against religious, educational, or recreational occupancy; and to make sure that a policy of title insurance has been issued for the protection of the owner. A competent attorney is essential for the proper adjudication of the matters discussed in this paragraph.

Have the physical aspects of the land been established sufficiently? All land ownership is circumscribed by limitations. The individual or corporate body which believes that the conveyance of a deed implies complete and unfettered possession is riding a blissful delusion.

All land, whether community-owned or church site, has its extremities. And these should be defined exactly. Wars are fought over the location of national borders — the law courts are inundated with actions stemming from disputed locations of boundaries between individual pieces of property. Prior to bidding, owner, architect, and contractors must have a positive and clear-cut concept of the location and dimensions of the property on which the proposed structure is to be located. This is established by deed descriptions, title search, and licensed survey.

It is the owner's responsibility to supply the architect with all information relating to property lines; the architect's to convey this information to bidders upon the contract documents.

The survey, in addition to the metes and bounds of the land, should show accurate topography and the location of public utilities. If subsurface information is available in the form of test pits or borings, this too should be added to the drawings and should be preserved as a matter of permanent record. Where trees are to be salvaged in the critical areas surrounding the building operation, the location and disposition of such trees should be included on the site plans.

The method of accepting bids from contractors may vary, and because of this it is well to discuss bidding rather early during the preparation of the final plans and specifications.

Methods for designating a contractor have varied since the first church foundation was laid, and even today there is wide diversity throughout the building industry in the selection of a contractor.

On the North American continent, because of great emphasis on competition, contractors are generally chosen on the basis of competitive lump sum bids. This method, which has undisputed advantages, also possesses certain built-in hazards which can be avoided under the guidance of an experienced architect.

Under the competitive bid system a number of bids are received from a number of contractors, each preferably selected on the basis of reputation, experience, and financial stability. If the bidders are thus prequalified and the bidding documents competently prepared, it generally follows that the estimates submitted are seriously developed and should not display excessive variation.

Where bidding is not restricted to known competence, irresponsibility may appear among the bidders, and the bids may vary dangerously. Temptation to accept the lowest bid is always present and always accompanied by potential risk.

When an extraordinarily low bid is received, it is Christian responsibility and good business judgment to give the low bidder an opportunity to review his cost sheets and, if he has made a mistake, permit him to withdraw his bid. He should not be allowed to modify his bid.

There is no legal obligation to award a contract to the lowest bidder, but where bids have been requested by a religious congregation from a list of acceptable bidders, there are important ethical pressures which dictate such an award to the willing qualified bidder whose competitive urge has enabled him to submit a successful bid.

Notwithstanding such established moral compulsions, it is prudent procedure that the owner be protected by a clause in the invitation to bids which gives him the right to reject any or all bids.

Like most competitive industry, the building business suffers periods of high mortality. The best general contractor may find himself in sudden financial jeopardy by reason of overextension, uncollectable accounts, or loss of borrowing ability. The architect and his client should be prepared to face this contingency as it arises, either through bid rejection or insistence on a protective bond.

Adversity can strike abruptly in the construction industry. It is quite possible that the contractor who qualified before bidding is less acceptable financially after the bids have been opened. There are several protective methods that may be utilized as safeguards against contractor's default. The first and most effective is a routine check by the architect into the low bidder's immediate financial position. Is he meeting his liabilities? What are his current assets? Does his bank consider him a good risk? Is he bondable?

Concurrently, a survey should be made of his immediate building operations. Is the progress continuous? Have any liens been filed? Are any of his subcontractors in default?

The answer to the last question is vital. More and more general contractors are gravitating away from the historic position of master builder with direct control over all trades in their own employ and, as a substitute, are acting as brokers or lumpers over a heterogeneous group of subcontractors — one for each trade.

It does not follow that a general contractor of the broker type is less qualified. His stature is established by his ability to employ and coordinate a group of subcontractors of sound financial standing and reputation. Review of the competence and financial standing of the major subcontractors by architect and owner is desirable.

But man for man, where a choice exists, one must choose the general contractor who employs his own tradesmen and who is directly responsible for his own excavation and foundation work, masonry, carpentry, and plastering. This is particularly true of church work, which is traditionally the field of the master builder, and where the standards for the basic trades are more exacting.

Although a prospective contractor may possess top rating, it is not prudent trusteeship to forgo the expense of performance and completion bonds. Omission of bonding should never occur by default. All aspects should be discussed in detail and the obvious hazards of no bond protection made known to the building committee and church governing body.

During the early stages of negotiation the protective benefits of the bond should be studied in detail, preferably under the guidance of an attorney or insurance broker experienced in bonding matters. The credentials of the company underwriting the bond should be scanned as closely as those of the contractor. A company overextended by reason of high claims should be avoided, as should those with a reputation for sidestepping valid obligations.

The precontract stages are time-consuming but not necessarily wasteful. During the interim period the architect and his consultants should be checking plans and specifications for errors or omissions, and where changes are under consideration these should be negotiated and added to the scope of the work before the signing of the contract.

Preliminary routine can become time-consuming and frustrating, particularly during seasons of good building weather. Where a feeling of mutual confidence exists, a letter of intent may be issued to the contractor by the architect upon authorization of the client. With such a letter in hand, the contractor can enter into firm commitments with his subcontractors, order basic materials, obtain permits, and arrange for insurance protection.

Insurance practices vary regionally, either by statute or local custom. The importance of proper protection cannot be overemphasized. Workmen's Compensation, public liability, property damage, and general coverage insurance are the fundamental classifications. In most areas it is customary for the contractor to carry Workmen's Compensation, property damage, and public liability insurance; for the owner to maintain general coverage insurance.

Policies should be drawn to protect the owner against third-party suits, and where there is a mortgagee the financing institution should be similarly protected.

In sections of the country subject to unusual weather the policy should include extended coverage protection against windstorm, flood, and so-called acts of God.

Because of the complicated nature of the building operation it is highly desirable that all insurance matters be reviewed mutually by agents for contractor and owner. The possibility exists that coverage may be inadequate or omitted entirely, or that the insurance company is unacceptable.

With all the preliminary work cared for, we are now at a point where the building operation can begin. All contract documents have been signed, building permits have been issued, insurance certificates reviewed, and ground has been broken.

All of these steps presuppose that the church governing body has made all necessary arrangements for adequate financing. It is customary for contractors to submit monthly requisitions for payment for work installed during the previous month. These are checked, corrected, and approved by the architect, and then sent to the owner for payment.

Payment procedures should be streamlined and totally devoid of red tape. The contractual obligation is clear for both sides: the contractor installs his work properly; the owner pays promptly.

The criteria for proper installation should be established by the architect and his supervisory staff. The extent of required supervision will vary from job to job. It is difficult to set hard and fast rules for supervision and inspection. One cannot overlook the fact that no general contractor is better than his subcontractor, no subcontractor better than his last mechanic at the end of the scaffold. Where a general contractor enjoys an established reputation for careful and continuous supervision over his own work, there the vigilance of the architect and owner can be more relaxed.

However, a greater burden will fall on the architect and owner where a contractor is not interested in the performance of his workmen. In more aggravated situations the full-time services of a clerk-of-the-work may be required. This man is employed by the architect, but his salary is reimbursed by the owner. In jobs long drawn out, the employment of the clerk-of-the-work can be costly. Most building operations run for about a year or perhaps longer. A competent clerk-of-the-work should be a man of extended experience and unchallengeable reputation. His salary over the space of a year could be a substantial addition to the overall cost of the job.

This fact should be given weight prior to the award of the contract. Preference should be given to the contractor with a reputation for coordinated and closely supervised work.

Supervision or inspection by members of the building committee or the congregation must be avoided. Supervision calls for extreme objectivity, a quality not always in evidence where individuals represent their church or their children. This does not mean that infractions noted by the building committee are to be disregarded. They should be brought to the attention of the architect, and resolved between architect and contractor.

Very few building operations are completed without some extra costs deriving from omissions, unforseen conditions, or voluntary changes requested by the congregation. This is an area in which Christian forbearance must manifest itself. Minor errors or inconsistencies may occur within the contract documents, foundation conditions may involve changes in design, the building committee may decide to include items not originally included within the scope of the operation. Normally such developments do not involve added cost of more than five percent, and it is a wise congregation indeed which sets up a contingency fund in anticipation of modifications.

All changes to the contract should be handled by the architect and should be in writing, either by letter or by formal change order, which spells out in full the extent of the departure. In fact, all transactions between the congregation and the contractor should be in writing. Oral agreements develop misunderstandings leading to recrimination and ending in litigation.

In order that rapport may continue among contractors, architect, and building committee, it may be desirable to hold a limited number of joint meetings during the period of construction. At these, questions relating to progress, workmanship, and completion can be discussed. Many potential misunderstandings can be averted through a sincere exchange of viewpoints. Like Solomon's temple, even the smallest church operation is a complexity involving the importation of materials from distant places. Given the proper opportunity, the intelligent contractor should be able to explain the reason for apparent delays which must attend the fabrication and delivery of structural specialties.

As the building approaches completion the architect and perhaps a selected member of the building committee will prepare so-called punch lists of items requiring completion or correction. This can be a laborious and time-consuming effort if held off too long. Obvious items should be corrected during the course of construction. It is unthinkable that basic structural corrections should appear upon the completion punch list.

As the structure approaches completion and dedication a welter of activities will develop, some of which may involve jurisdictional labor disputes. Not all church furniture manufacturers and very few organ builders are associated with organized labor. Very often these facilities are purchased apart from the general construction contract. If the completion schedule of the building requires that nonaffiliated and organized trades work side by side, trouble and delay may ensue. The pattern will vary across the nation depending on the attitude and strength of entrenched labor.

It is advisable that the situation be discussed at an early date among all parties involved. If uncertainties are evident it would be preferable to have all general construction completed in its entirety before the furniture and organ installations are started.

Organ builders are sensitive to the character of finishing materials and are particularly partial to reflective surfaces which impart an acoustical brilliance to the interior. Within reasonable limits and where no sizable extra costs are involved, their recommendations should be incorporated. It is far more preferable, however, if architect and organ builder are exposed to each other during the preliminary planning stages. Most organ builders have definite requirements about organ location and church construction and finish which cannot possibly be fulfilled at the last moment.

The place of the pastor has not been related herein to the building operation. To the newly ordained clergyman plunged into congregational life the added burden of a new building invokes situations calling on the patience and resourcefulness of a superman. At best, building construction is dirty, inefficient, and cumbersome. At its worst it presents undesirable frustrations to all concerned and most particularly to the pastor of the church.

Where a pastor is constitutionally unequal to the realities and profanities of the building site, there is yet much that he can contribute. A building operation has been described, without exaggeration, as a sea of mud bounded by a crisis on all four sides. Here the quiet Christian approach can calm the troubled waters and soothe ruffled tempers. The pastor can render a most important service if he chooses the role of Christian arbiter instead of being pushed into the position of uninitiated clerk-of-the-work by some aggressive member of the congregation.

It must not be forgotten that in spite of all the vicissitudes every building is at some time completed. How much better if it is occupied in an atmosphere of quiet Christian dignity.

Let us not forget that no parish program is better than its architect, no architect better than the contractor, no contractor better than the craftsman; all will need the prayers of pastor and congregation.

Of such is the Kingdom.

photographs

First Lutheran Church, Brookings, S. Dak.

The Cerny Associates, Inc., A. I. A., Architects, St. Paul, Minn.

Increasing importance placed on Christian education has produced many noteworthy church educational structures. Many older churches have been confronted with inadequate sites to accommodate this increasing emphasis. However, the direct solution illustrated indicates an adequate site combined with a simple, economical solution.

Protestant Chapel, Brandeis University, Waltham, Mass.

Harrison and Abramovitz, A. I. A., Architects, New York, N. Y.

Can today's church contribute importantly to today's architecture, as did the church in ages past? Can contemporary architecture meet the spiritual needs and economic limitations of today's church, as did the design of the Colonial meeting house and the Gothic cathedral? This chapel, one of three (Catholic, Protestant, and Jewish) at one of the United States' newest planned universities, offers convincing proof that contemporary architecture, using such modern materials as plate glass, can create a really beautiful church.

St. Mark's Episcopal Church, Oenoke Ridge, New Canaan, Conn.

Sherwood, Mills and Smith, A. I. A., Architects, Stamford, Conn.

This fresh interior has a striking accent at the chancel — a wood and metal reredos in front of the choir, featuring some 350 copper and brass sculptured figures, designed by Clark Fitz-Gerald, sculptor, of Castine, Maine. The combination of interior materials provides a quality effective to producing a worshipful atmosphere.

Faith Salem United Church of Christ, St. Louis, Mo.

Frederick W. Dunn, F. A. I. A., Architect, St. Louis, Mo.

Mr. Dunn, in collaboration with Emil Frei Associates, by using new glass techniques developed the striking effect of this glass wall with a north exposure. The design concept for this modest church plant was established around it.

St. Paul's Episcopal Cathedral, Peoria, Ill.

Frederick W. Dunn, F. A. I. A., Architect, St. Louis, Mo.

With extraordinary skill the architect has employed the use of various artists and artisans to emphasize the many elements of the Episcopal liturgy in the interior of this church. Zelda Strecher designed the acoustical reredos behind the altar; William Donaldson designed the carpeting, which was woven in Puerto Rico; and Emil Frei Associates designed the stained-glass windows. Each detail of church furnishings is designed with care and restraint by the architect, adding to the cohesive character of the whole.

PEORIA STAR-JOURNAL

Chapel for St. Stephen's Episcopal School Near Austin, Tex.

Fehr and Granger, A. I. A., Architects, Austin, Tex.

This is an excellent example of the altar located at the crossing of the transepts and the nave, with a combination of basic materials forming the framework of the composition. Brick floors, native stone, ashular walls, exposed structural steel beam roof, and wood deck. Altar appointments are basic, with individual chairs used instead of pews. The chairs give an openness of arrangement and space worthy of more usage in the United States than the more commonly used pews.

Danforth Chapel, Colorado State University, Fort Collins, Colo.

James M. Hunter, F. A. I. A., and Associates, Architects, Boulder, Colo.

The copper doors designed by Lynn Wolfe are an active element in the design of this engaging little chapel where the copper color contrasts with the white native sandstone of the masonry walls and the deep-red flagstone walks. The close cooperation of the artist and architect is evident in the successful integration of this work of art, despite a moderate budget, and allays the common concept that a work of art is a luxury article in a church building.

Danforth Chapel, Colorado State University, Fort Collins, Colo.

James M. Hunter, F.A.I.A., and Associates, Architects, Boulder, Colo.

The basic structure of this small chapel, accommodating persons and used by students and faculty of this agricultu and mechanical college, is simple and direct, contributing quiet and private meditation for all denominational belie Indigenous materials of white native sandstone for mason walls, deep-red flagstone floors, and natural fir roof and w dow walls all contribute to its dignified atmosphere and d tinctive appearance.

St. Augustine's Episcopal Church, Gary, Ind.

Edward D. Dart, A.I.A., Architect, Chicago, Ill.

The significant simplicity of the exterior of this small church carried dramatically into the interior, where a low narth leads into a sweepingly high nave of pleasing proportio Chancel furnishings of equal simplicity give emphasis to t corpus over the altar. Permanent seating is 240, with a ch loft of 25 and a study, sacristy, and robing room behind t altar wall.

Chapel at Illinois Institute of Technology, Chicago, Ill.

Mies Van Der Rohe, F.A.I.A., Architect, Chicago, Ill.

The philosophy of the architect, "Less is more," is well exemplified in this small, direct chapel building. Each element of the composition contributes to the success of the whole. The chapel itself is part of a much larger composition of other new buildings by the same architect in the same direct character and using the same materials. This directness of approach is very difficult to achieve, although it may appear effortless to the average person.

St. Mark's Episcopal Church, New Canaan, Conn.

Sherwood, Mills and Smith, A.I.A., Architects, Stamford, Co

This interior chancel screen, designed by Clark Fitz-Ger of Castine, Maine, displays the apt blending of the skills artist, craftsmen, and architects in meeting the liturgical ne of the church.

F. R. DAPPRICH

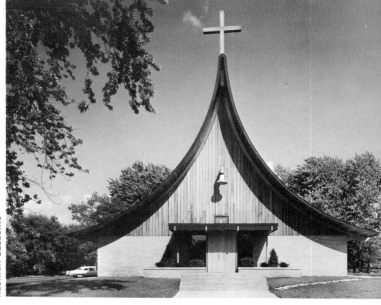

HEDRICH-BLESSING

St. Augustine's Episcopal Church, Gary, Ind.

The form of this small church is fresh and creative without being theatrical, as happens too often. This simplicity of character will survive the test of time, which is the only judge of good architecture.

Oneonta Congregational Church, South Pasadena, Calif.

Smith, Powell & Morgridge, A. I. A., Architects, Los Angeles

This interior is traditional in form, taking a halfway position between past and present, while at the same time successfully combining stateliness and grace.

**Chapel, Concordia Senior College, The Lutheran Church
Missouri Synod, Fort Wayne, Ind.**

Eero Saarinen, F. A. I. A., Architect

This chapel is the focal point, both functionally and esthetic
for a new college campus where the creation of an envir
ment was sought appropriate to the intellectual and spirit
training of young men who would go on to professional stu
in theology. The central chapel in a village concept
developed to achieve this quiet, unified environment. The h
pitched roof in contrast to the low pitch of surrounding bu
ings gives the significant note. Rich materials of speci
made brick of diamond pattern, a new roofing tile, cop
trim, and a strong stone base enhance the effect.

In the all-important college chapel the desired atmosphere
worship was achieved by numerous means — the lofty sl
of the enclosing roof sets the place apart from the outs
world; light filters up from below through a fixed horizo
sash set between side-aisle baffles; along the full length
the ridge is a continuous peak skylight. Floodlighting
altar and the aluminum cross mounted on the diamond-sha
brick wall at the east end is a full-height roof skylight insta
in the south roof slope.

Lutheran Church, Portland, Oreg.

o Belluschi, F. A. I. A., Architect, Cambridge, Mass.

is church the architect, with Frederic Littman as sculptor,
designed a fresh accent to the building in the low-relief
er doors of simple beauty and religious significance. This
ch with its integrated works of art derives its strength from
simple directness which eschews the gimmick, structural
ecorative.

lren's Chapel of the Neighborhood Church, dena, Calif.

and Williams, A. I. A., Architects, Pasadena, Calif.

chapel scaled down to child size is a full-fledged member
e family, standing alone yet linked with the others in
ouping around pleasant little courts and gardens. The
ing retains a family resemblance with the other struc-
by using the same red wood exterior and earth colors
e general scheme, but retaining its own freshness.

▼

JULIUS SHULMAN

The Church of the Redeemer, Baltimore, Md.

Pietro Belluschi, F. A. I. A., and Rogers, Taliaferro, Kostritsky and Lamb, A. I. A., Associated Architects, Cambridge, Mass., and Baltimore, Md.

This church of significant form, based on an expressive structural system and materials use, has its chancel placed forward into the main body of the church and becomes a three-sided platform. In the Episcopalian tradition sacramental worship — the altar — is considered as important as preaching and the reading of the Scriptures — pulpit and lectern. The dual emphasis shared by God's Word and the Sacrament is clearly expressed in the plan. The altar takes its place in the midst of the worshiping congregation; pulpit and lectern occupy positions on either side at the rear corners of the chancel.

St. George's Episcopal Church, Durham, N. H

Carter and Woodruff, A. I. A., Architects, Nashua, N. H

This small church, seating 150, on the principal stree of a small university town effectively demonstrates the essentia ingredient of a strong but simple design concept sympatheti to the liturgy of the Episcopal Church The stained glass, the pink and gray granite, and the cedar of the exterior achieve a remarkable unity at a modest budget. Small churches need not be ordinary in concept but can be outstanding as a community and spiritual asset through proper study of the problem and competent professional guidance